DEATH OF A DON

A Mystery/Comedy in Two Acts

by Ronald Krine Myroup

SAMUEL FRENCH, INC.

45 West 25th Street   NEW YORK 10010
7623 Sunset Boulevard HOLLYWOOD 90046
LONDON   TORONTO

IMPORTANT BILLING AND CREDIT REQUIREMENTS

All producers of DEATH OF A DON *must* give credit to the Author of the Play in all programs distributed in connection with performances of the Play and in all instances in which the title of the Play appears for purposes of advertising, publicizing or otherwise exploiting the Play and/or a production. The name of the Author *must* also appear on a separate line, on which no other name appears, immediately following the title, and *must* appear in size of type not less than fifty percent the size of the title type.

CHARACTERS

CONNIE ELAINE GIOVANI: The Don's eldest daughter is a tough woman. With looks like Sophia Loren and a business mind like Michael Corleone she is an asset to her father's organization. At 33 the Don decides she must marry a man of his choosing, not hers. This does not make her happy.

ROCKY STUDDS MALONE: The Don's arch enemy and the young leader of a new mob that is trying to bring back the glamour of the mafia. He would do anything to bump off the Don for two reasons: he and Connie are secretly in love; and his death would pave the way for Malone's new era.

BABY GIOVANI: The Don's youngest daughter sings like a song bird and eats more pasta than the entire island of Sicily. She is about 17, very cute, but very pudgy. Baby aspires to be a Broadway singer, but her father prevents this. Like her father she, too, has a mean streak.

CORRITA GIOVANI: The Don's long-suffering wife. After being married to him for forty years she's had enough of the old ways. Black dresses, constant prayer and no family vacations have worn her down. She wants a change, but she knows that's impossible, at least while her husband lives.

ROBERTO GIOVANI: The Don's youngest son is twenty-ish and an egghead nerd. His father has said "Itza bad enough you gotta be pansy, but youa gotta be nerd too?" Roberto wants to be left alone so he can write poetry, but the Don teases and torments him. Everyone has a breaking point, even nerds.

VALARIA CONSTANTINE: The Don's ex-mistress, and now current girlfriend of his oldest son, knows too much. One of the dying breed of glamour molls, this hot tomato is determined to see that justice prevails. Dating her ex-lover's son is her only way of getting back at the Don for dumping her.

GINO GIOVANI: The eldest son of the Don is in his late 30's. He wants to turn the family business into a legal enterprise—the numbers racket. Phone numbers, that is. He wants to get in on the 976 craze that's hit the nation. He can't do this because his father clings to the old ways.

DONALD GIOVANI: The last godfather is 70 and very tired. All of his friends have been either rubbed out by rival gangs or imprisoned for life. However, he's refused to let go of the old traditions. He's a bitter, flustered old man in a time warp. He would die if he knew who murdered him.

ONE-EYED JOE PROVOLONE: Connie's pre-arranged husband. He's a little balding on top, a little wide around the middle and a little long in tooth. He's a mafia patsy and terrified of his new bride.

TIME & PLACE

The present.
Donald Giovani's study.

ACT I

Scene 1

SCENE: An elegant, symmetrical study. Beginning STAGE LEFT—an angled wall borders DOWNSTAGE to UPSTAGE and contains two large windows. UPSTAGE LEFT wall—two floor-to-ceiling bookcases. UPSTAGE CENTER—five small steps leading to French doors, an exit to the rest of the house. UPSTAGE RIGHT wall also has two bookcases with angled wall and windows following. STAGE RIGHT and LEFT are mirrors of each other. DOWNSTAGE LEFT there is a huge walnut desk with a throne-like chair and a globe off to the side. DOWNSTAGE CENTER has an oriental carpet. DOWNSTAGE RIGHT has a leather sofa and a coffee table. In the UPSTAGE RIGHT corner a Tiffany floor lamp proudly stands. Also DOWNSTAGE RIGHT, and behind the sofa, a small bar is against one of the windows. NOTE: There is a secret panel that opens outward in the lower portion of the STAGE LEFT bookcase. It is activated by the pulling of a certain book.

AT RISE: The French doors swing open revealing CONNIE GIOVANI on her knees having just picked the lock. Clad in a tight-fitting red dress SHE cautiously enters and goes to the bar looking for a drink. SHE bends over to look in the cabinet beneath the bar.

7

ROCKY STUDDS MALONE enters from the secret panel in STAGE LEFT bookcase. HE is dashing, well-built and lives up to his middle name. As HE puts a white carnation in the lapel of his fashionable suit, ROCKY smiles at Connie's posterior.

ROCKY. Abondanza!

(CONNIE turns around and the CHARACTERS slowly stalk each.)

ROCKY. (*Sensual.*) Connie Elaine Giovani, I LOVE YOU!

CONNIE. (*Breathless.*) Say it again.

ROCKY. I LOVE YOU!

CONNIE. Louder.

ROCKY. (*Building.*) I LOVE YOU! I love you more than life. I love you to death. Rocky Studds Malone loves Connie Elaine Giovani.

(SHE smiles devilishly. THEY kiss.)

ROCKY. How much time do we have?

CONNIE. (*Moves away from Rocky, suddenly depressed.*) Until the Don finds me a husband. Three weeks tops.

ROCKY. (*Taking jacket off.*) No. I mean now. Today. Do we got time to ...

CONNIE. (*Interrupting.*) They're throwing a surprise birthday party for the son-of-a-bitch in a half an hour.

ROCKY. Connie. Man, I can't take it no more. I feel like I'm dating somebody from the witness protection program.

CONNIE. There's nothing wrong with our relationship the way it is.

ROCKY. No? All the broads in the world and I gotta fall in love with the daughter of Don Giovani. ~~Jesus, Mary and Joseph.~~

CONNIE. It'll be a lot harder to see each other when I get married.

ROCKY. Any idea who it's gonna be?

CONNIE. Papa's interviewing grooms with Nick the Fish.

ROCKY. I heard.

CONNIE. So far he ain't found nobody he wants as a son-in-law.

ROCKY. Your father is a cruel man. He knows he can end the feud between the Giovani family and the Malone family at any time. You said you were gonna convince him to merge our families, Connie.

CONNIE. I've been busy!

ROCKY. I'm beginning to think you like being the business advisor to your family.

CONNIE. (*Totally honest.*) I do, but I love you. You know that. You're more important to me than the business.

ROCKY. Any woman in this neighborhood would give her right arm to be my wife.

CONNIE. (*Sarcastic.*) Is that what you want? A woman without an arm?

ROCKY. ~~Jesus, Joseph and Mary.~~ Cv-o-35

CONNIE. Don't get religious on me, Rocky. Look ... I want to be your wife.

ROCKY. We got no solution here, Connie. I love you. You love me. Your father and his gang are my enemies. You work for him. He depends on you. I want you to work for me. I want you in my house.

CONNIE. Yeah, well as long the son-of-a-bitch is alive we keep doing the Romeo and Juliet bit.

ROCKY. I'm getting tired of it, Connie.

CONNIE. (*Snap.*) Deal with it!

ROCKY. (*Slow.*) And what if I don't want to no more?

CONNIE. (*Screaming.*) So, dump me. (*SHE begins hitting the side of his head.*) Walk outta my life. See if I care. But don't think there aren't enough men willing to give up their body parts for a date with Connie Elaine Giovani. (*CONNIE moves to the other side of the stage. Silence.*)

ROCKY. I hate this hiding and ducking around corners crap. If your old man was ...

CONNIE. (*Interrupting.*) Don't even think it. What did you promise me?

ROCKY. You know I'd never do it, Connie.

CONNIE. Promise!

ROCKY. I never broke a promise to you.

CONNIE. I wanna hear it!

ROCKY. I promise I will never kill your father. (*Pause, emotional.*) I love you, Connie. I love you so much.

CONNIE. I know. Come here.

(ROCKY rushes to Connie—THEY embrace.)

ROCKY. I need you so much, baby.
CONNIE (*Weak.*) Oh, Rocky ...

*(THEY kiss passionately until a NOISE is heard outside
the study doors.)*

BABY. (*Offstage.*) He locked it again, Mama!
CORRITA. (*Offstage.*) Get outta my way, Baby! I gotta
a hair pin. Move.
ROCKY. (*Whispering.*) I love you. I love you more
than anything.
CONNIE. (*Whispering.*) I know. Someday I'm gonna
figure out why we play this love/hate game.

*(ROCKY goes to secret panel, stops, turns and throws her
a kiss. SHE smiles as HE disappears behind the panel.)*

CORRITA. (*Offstage.*) Baby. You ina my damn light.
Move!
CONNIE. *(Softly.)* And there I am—where is my
Romeo?

*(The study door opens. CORRITA is on her knees just
finishing picking the lock. SHE is dressed in black, hair
pulled back. Throughout the play CORRITA is never
without her black purse. CORRITA stands. BABY is
carrying a cake and presents. SHE wears a larger version
of the dress made famous by Marilyn Monroe in* The
Seven Year Itch. *THEY enter and are shocked to find
Connie.)*

CORRITA. Forty years of marriage and the Don donna give me no key to this room. (*To Connie.*) What the hell are you doin' here?

(*CONNIE crosses to Corrita and kisses her. BABY sets the cake on the desk and gets the presents.*)

CONNIE. Howya doin', Mama? You look old.

CORRITA. I said what are you doin' here?

CONNIE. I come here to think. Okay?

CORRITA. Use the bathroom like everybody else. You no belong ina your papa's study.

BABY. Hi, Connie. Guess what I got the Don for his birthday?

CONNIE. Oh, God. You're gonna sing for him again.

(*CORRITA spreads a red and white checkered tablecloth over the desk. CONNIE crosses to the sofa and sits.*)

CORRITA. (*Warning.*) Connie.

BABY. I'm gonna a song I wrote for him.

CONNIE. (*Mock shock.*) No!

BABY. I'm gonna sing it like Marilyn Monroe. You know like this. (*Breathy like Marilyn.*)
I say. I say. I say Happy Birthday, Mister Daddy.

CONNIE. Yeah. That was right before JFK died, huh? Maybe we get lucky and the Don gets killed too.

CORRITA. CONNIE!

CONNIE. Sorry, Mama. I keep thinking about Papa's pre-arranged marriage crap. It gets me. It gets me right ... (*Gestures to her gut. BABY crosses to Connie.*) ... here, Mama. (*To Baby.*) What do you want?

BABY. (*Twirling around.*) What do you think of the dress?

CONNIE. I think the Weight Watcher's diet hasn't helped very much.

CORRITA. Connie, I don't like thisa mood you ina. Apollo-guys to you sister.

CONNIE. I'm sorry ... (*Pause.*) ... that you're a size twenty, a compulsive eater and a lousy singer.

(*BABY goes to the nearest corner to pout.*)

CORRITA. CONNIE!!!! What's a matter for you?

CONNIE. (*Yelling.*) I don't wanna marry a man chosen by somebody named Nick the Fish!

CORRITA. Don't take it out on your sister. Look! Do youa think I had a choice when I wasa your age?

CONNIE. Your life is over. Mine is just beginning. I'll always know where my husband is by the delicate fragrance of yesterday's catch.

CORRITA. Papa only wants the best for you, Connie.

CONNIE. Only 'cause I'm the best damn advisor the family has ever had.

CORRITA. Please, Connie. Your papa is seventy today. Please make nice for him.

(*ROBERTO appears at the door with bags of potato chips, two jars of nuts and baskets. HE is wearing thick glasses and "out of date" clothing. He's not handsome.*)

ROBERTO. A pot on the stove is boiling over, Mama.

CORRITA.Connie, go save the Cioppino.

CONNIE. (*Disgusted.*) Fish soup!

CORRITA. It's tradition. You're gonna have to learn how to cooka it too. You'll be a wife soon.

CONNIE (*Walking to study door.*) What the hell is a matter with this family! Didja all sleep through the sixties? Women are free.

CORRITA. In this family women are free ... to cook, clean and have babies. Now get outta here.

(*As CONNIE exits BABY comes back to the action, but not before SHE gives Connie's back an Italian gesture flicked from her chin.*)

ROBERTO. Mama, I was up half the night writing this poem for Papa. Why can't I read it?

CORRITA. (*Taking the baskets and food.*) Why isn't Gino here? I asked him to be on time.

ROBERTO. Mama, you ain't listening to me.

CORRITA. What do you suppose will happen if I leta you read thisa poem to you Papa?

ROBERTO. He'll hear the words of love I have written for him and he will understand them and by understanding them he will understand me in all my complexities.

CORRITA. Your papa kills people for a living. Don't you understand that? Roberto! He's a racketeer, a rat and up to his neck in the old family honor system.

ROBERTO. My poem can change that.

CORRITA. Darling, not evena the FBI canna change that.

ROBERTO. So, I can't read my poem?

CORRITA. (*Screaming.*) Whadda youa? DEAF? Donna you understand nothing? He's a son-of-a-bitch who makes your life miserable when you talk about this poetry crap. Why'da ya do it, son?

BABY. Mama, calm down. The veins in your neck are sticking out.

CORRITA. Maybe they should pop out and I should die, then everybody would be happy, God forbid.

ROBERTO. Mama, I'm sorry.

CORRITA. (*Calmer.*) It's not youa fault you weren't born more like your older brother and a little less like Don Knotts. Please, Roberto, stay outta Papa's striking distance, huh?

ROBERTO. Can I read YOU my poem?

BABY. And then I'll, like, sing for you.

CORRITA. (*Throws her hands into the air in despair and wails.*) Oh, God ina heaven. Where did I go wrong?

BABY. Aren't you proud of us, Mama?

CORRITA. Yes, but I don't count. Your papa wanted alla his kiddies to follow ina his footprints. He wanted kids who kill at the drop of a hat—not William Shakespeare and Barbra Streisand.

BABY. But he likes my singing.

CORRITA. Yes. When you do it at weddings and funerals. He donna like the idea of you going professional.

BABY. (*Takes CENTER STAGE.*) I'm gonna be a famous singer someday. I'm gonna scale the heights of the music industry. I wanna sign autographs and have my picture on the cover of *National Enquirer*. I wanna be so famous they ask me to sing at the Pizza Bowl.

(ROBERTO breaks into an applause.)

BABY. (*Caught up in her own world.*) I want my name in lights. (*Shaking her whole body.*) BA-BY GIO-VANI LI-VE!

CORRITA. Baby Giovani DEAD, if Papa finds outta you went to that audition.

BABY. I got the part, didn't I?

ROBERTO. Imagine, Baby, if you and me both become famous. Me, the next Shakespeare. You, the next Madonna.

BABY. (*Like a prayer.*) Madonna!

CORRITA. (*Wailing.*) Oh, God in heaven.

BABY. You say that a lot, Mama.

CORRITA. You'll say it too when you're a parent. And may I live to see that day.

CONNIE. (*Appears at the study door holding a steaming pot.*) Roberto, get this damn thing outta my life.

(*ROBERTO runs up to her and removes the pot. HE places it on the desk. CONNIE goes to the sofa and falls into it.*)

ROBERTO. Guess what I got for Papa, Connie.

CONNIE. Oh, God. You wrote him another poem. Why do you keep trying?

ROBERTO. I love him, Connie.

CONNIE. He hates you.

CORRITA. (*Scolding.*) CONNIE!

CONNIE. It's the truth, Mama. The sooner Roberto realizes Papa hates his guts the sooner we can get him into therapy. (*Pause.*) Read your poem to me, Roberto.

ROBERTO. Really?

CONNIE. Yeah. Go ahead. God only knows Papa ain't gonna wanna hear it.

ROBERTO. (*Takes CENTER STAGE.*)

I don't think I have ever seen a thing as lovely as a dad.

Even during those times when you slugged me 'cause I was bad.

I know you think you hate me and wish I'd go far away.

But I'm here ready and willing to wish you a happy birthday.

In man's soul there is space for music and love.

For the finer things in life and the magic of God above.

There's also a place deep in your heart

For my special brand of art.

You are a good papa—kind and ultra cool

Now, please gimme the money for poetry school.

CORRITA. (*Wailing.*) Oh, God in heaven. Where did I go wrong?

CONNIE (*To Corrita—bitchy.*) You married Papa. (*To Roberto.*) That was nice, pet. Now go and make your favorite sister a drink.

(*ROBERTO runs to the bar and makes a drink and will hand it to Connie when finished. BABY takes CENTER STAGE.*)

BABY. Now, I suppose youse are all wondering how I'm gonna pull off a Marilyn Monroe impression. Well, I rented all her movies and I've been watching 'em, see. It ain't original or anything, but I think it's something he's gonna remember for the rest of his life.

CONNIE. And probably well into his after life.

BABY. (*Ignoring Connie.*) I thought this dress looked the best on my figure and of course youse all know what movie it's from. (*BABY lifts her dress up like the scene from* The Seven Year Itch.)

CONNIE. Roberto, make it a double.

BABY. (*Undaunted, runs up the study steps.*) I'm gonna walk down the steps slowly with a look on my face like I'm happy, but sexy.

(*BABY contorts her face in a failed attempt to look sexy and begins singing her own song. Her Marilyn Monroe accent is over-dramatic. Concurrent, CONNIE starts talking loudly.*)

BABY. (*Singing.*)
I say. I say. I say.
Happy Birthday, Mister Daddy.
I pray. I pray. I pray.
You have a good day,
    Oh dear Daddy.
My way. My way. My way.
For your to have a good day
is to say
Happy Birthday …

CONNIE. (*To Roberto.*) Roberto, I think you are by far the most talented member of this otherwise untalented family. You have the soul of Browning, the wit of Byron, the heart of Shakespeare and the face of Mel Brooks. (*Pause.*) You're a regular poetic Frankenstein.

BABY. (*Stops singing and yells.*) HEY! I'm singing over here.

CONNIE. Is that what it is? And here I was ready to call 911 thinking someone was in pain.

(GINO GIOVANI appears in the study door. VALARIA CONSTANTINE is with him.)

GINO. You shouldn't talk to Baby like that.

BABY. *(SHE thinks the world of Gino.)* GINO!

GINO. *(Tosses a spray can of whipped cream to Baby.)* Here, Baby, a little reminder how much I love your singing.

BABY. *(Catches it, opens it and sprays some whipped cream into her mouth.)* My favorite. Did you like my song?

GINO. Yeah, Baby. It was okay. *(To Connie.)* Why do you tease her?

CONNIE. Why does the sun rise every morning?

GINO. Man, you got a smart answer for everything, don't cha?

CONNIE. The Don don't like how you handled the Cartier job. He thinks you're goin' soft. Youse left all the bank employees alive. Witnesses talk. Witnesses point fingers.

(GINO goes to the bar and fixes a drink. CORRITA checks out Valaria and rolls her eyes.)

GINO. Papa don't think a job can be pulled without spilling buckets of blood. But he's wrong—dead wrong.

VALARIA. Ain't you gonna introduce me to your family, Gino?

GINO. Hey! Everybody that's Valaria Constantine. She's my ... uh ... date.

VALARIA. (*Loud and rehearsed.*) I'm pleased to meet all of you. What a lovely fortress you got here.

GINO. (*Crosses to Corrita and tries to kiss her.*) Yo, Mama.

CORRITA. (*Angry. Shoving a bowl of pecans at Gino.*) NUTS.

GINO. Brrrrrr. A little cold in here. What's the ...?

CORRITA. (*Interrupting.*) You're late, big shot.

GINO. I ain't been in the house two minutes and you're shoving nuts in my face.

CORRITA. You too smart for you own good and you know what I'm talking about, big shot.

GINO. I never know what you're talking about. When's the old man getting here?

CORRITA. (*Builds.*) Your PAPA will be here any minute. I'm sick and tired all youse complaining about him. He's the one who's supported this family for the last forty years. I don't wanta anything happening that might upset him. He's seventy today and I want him to have a good time—even if it kills all of you. Roberto go be a lookout for the Don. He gonna be here any minute, God forbid.

(ROBERTO *goes to study door and waits. The tension between GINO and CONNIE builds as their sibling ritual is played out. THEY stare at each other as GINO takes out a cigarette and lights it, prompting CONNIE to do the same. CONNIE downs her drink in one shot. GINO also.*)

GINO. (*To Valaria.*) Get me another drink.
CONNIE. (*To Baby.*) I need a refill too.

(*BABY and VALARIA take their glasses and run to bar. CONNIE crosses and sits on the sofa. GINO crosses and sits in a reception chair.*)

CONNIE. (*To Gino.*) I was writing the paychecks today. Why'd Toehead Verelli get an extra G for rubbing out Judge McClure?
GINO. Toehead took out the D.A. too.
CONNIE. One bullet, two birds?
GINO. The bullet went right "true" both of 'em.

(*BABY and VALARIA fight over the bottle of vodka.*)

CONNIE. (*Sarcastic.*) We're giving Toehead an extra thousand cause the Judge's bullet just happened to get in way of the D.A.'s life? Why should our man get paid extra for doing what he was paid to do in the first place?
GINO. It's my new job incentive program.
CONNIE. This is the mob, Gino, not a Howard Johnson's restaurant.

(*BABY and VALARIA run to serve their drinks.*)

GINO. A happy employee is a good employee.
CONNIE. Where do you come up with these stupid ideas?
GINO. I read the *Wall Street Journal*. Whadda you kicking for? He killed the judge and the D.A. with the same bullet. He deserved that extra dough.

CONNIE. He deserved a pat on the back for not wasting a second bullet. That's all.

GINO. I'm helping morale.

CONNIE. You're helping the family to the poorhouse.

GINO. If the Don would listen to my idea the family wouldn't ever have to worry about money again.

CONNIE. Don't start with that 976 bullshit again.

GINO. Connie, what the hell is with you? Why don't you listen?

CONNIE. (*Hits Gino's head.*) You got nothing up here. 976 numbers is for horny people not mobsters.

(VALARIA starts picking her teeth with a credit card. Disgusted, CONNIE watches her.)

GINO. It's the wave of the future. 976 numbers are gonna bring in millions. I know.

CONNIE. How can you know? You don't even know how to pick up women? (*Indicating Valaria.*) Where'd you get her? K-mart?

VALARIA. Where's the john?

CONNIE. AHHHH! A blue light special.

GINO. (*To Valaria.*) HOLD IT! (*To Connie.*) Like you know everything about men. Huh? Like you pick the right ones. Say, why don't you bring your lover boy home to meet the Don over Mama's manicotti. We all know, Connie, and we think it's a disgrace.

CONNIE. You really are a bastard.

CORRITA. (*Screaming.*) What is this? A scene from King Lear? Shut-upa both of youse. Talk business at the office not ina my home. It's the Don's birthday and youse all gonna have a good time. 'Cause if I could survive forty

years of sharing the same bed with that ~~son-of-a-bitch~~
you canna survive "tree" hours on his birthday—
~~GODDAMN~~! *4 words of Italian*

ROBERTO. He's here. He's here. He's coming.
Shhhhhhhhh.

CORRITA. (*Happy.*) Okay. Everybody hide, now. He's
coming, God forbid.

(*EVERYONE scatters and hides. ITALIAN MUSIC
begins. DON enters. HE is gray looking and walks
down the steps of the study slowly. When he reaches
the last step THEY jump out and scream "SURPRISE."
Startled, the DON jumps back, suddenly grabs his heart
and goes into heart attack spasms—flailing from one
end of the study to the other. Finally, HE lands in the
sofa, apparently dead. Neck-breaking speed, panic and,
in some cases, happiness ensue. BABY and ROBERTO
go to the Don. CORRITA stands nearby.*)

ROBERTO. Oh, my God! Oh, my God! Oh, my God!
CORRITA. Naw, it couldn't be that easy.
CONNIE. Is he dead? Is he dead?
ROBERTO. Papa! Papa! Speak to me. Speak! Speak!
BABY. He's not a dog, Roberto!
CORRITA. Naw, it couldn't be that easy.
VALARIA. Want me to give him mouth to mouth?
CONNIE. (*To Valaria.*) Slut!
BABY. (*Crying.*) PAPA!!!!!!

(*GINO runs to the phone and dials. BABY begins wailing
with sobs and tears.*)

CONNIE. What if he ain't fully dead? Shouldn't we ... hit him with something.

ROBERTO. CONNIE!

CONNIE. I mean, to put him out of his misery.

CORRITA. Connie, go check and see if he's really, really dead?

CONNIE. Who am I, Marcus Welby?

GINO. (*Into phone.*) Toehead, it's Gino. Get on the horn to the 976 organization. Yes, now, today.

ROBERTO. (*Crying.*) Oh, God, Papa's dead. He's dead. Oh, God. We killed him. We did.

BABY. Oh, God. What are we going to do? We killed Papa.

VALARIA. Shouldn't someone call 911?

CONNIE. (*To Valaria.*) Shut-up!

GINO. (*Into the phone.*) The Don is dead.

CONNIE. Oh, how I dreamt of this moment.

ROBERTO. (*Suddenly stops crying.*) Does this mean I can go to poetry school, Mama?

BABY. (*Singing.*) I say. I say. I say ...

CORRITA. SHUT UP YOU FACES! He ain't even cold and listen to youse. A man is dead here. Show some respect. Your papa isa gone, but not forgotten. He wasn't always a son-of-a-bitch, you know. He had good points. (*Thinks for two or three beats.*) I can't think of any right now, but that don't matter. Your papa was a gentleman. He treated me ... okay. I loved him ... for the first twenty years or so. He ... never hit me. Then again, he never took me to Disney World. (*Getting angry.*) Everything we own is stolen. Everything I've ever worn has been bought with blood money. He's treated me like a second class citizen all my life. (*Attacks the Don and strangles him.*) I've made over ten million tons of pasta FOR THIS SON-OF-A-BITCH!!!!

(The DON opens his eyes. CORRITA screams. The DON grabs Corrita by the neck yelling.)

THE DON. You've made over ten million tons of the worst pasta I ever had to eat.

(The DON tosses CORRITA on the sofa and stands up. The DON goes CENTER STAGE.)

CORRITA. I didn't think it was gonna be that easy.

GINO. *(Into phone.)* Never mind. It lives.

CONNIE. *(To the Don.)* You can't do anything right, can you?

ROBERTO. *(Runs to the Don and showers him with hugs and kisses.)* It's a miracle!

THE DON. *(Pushes him away.)* Don't be kissing me, pansy.

(The FAMILY forms a semi-circle behind the DON as he makes his speech.)

THE DON. Youse all waiting for me to die like vultures. Rocky Studds Malone and his gang wanna see me dead too. I expected more outta my own family. You don't know what tradition means. *(To Connie.)* Get diz true your fat head. You gonna marry who I say you gonna marry. *(To Gino.)* 976! SORRY WRONG NUMBER! We're hoods. We kill people who get in our way as we make money illegally.

GINO. Then you'd love this 976 racket. It's got ...

THE DON. (*Slaps Gino across the head.*) SHUT-UP. (*To Roberto.*) Hey, you, pansy. Come here.

(*ROBERTO comes to the Don. The DON gets him in a headlock. ROBERTO's arms are flailing.*)

THE DON. How can you be a poet when you don't know how to kill nobody? Besides, your poems stink. Get on your knees.

(*ROBERTO drops to his knees. BABY dances up to the DON knowing she is his favorite.*)

BABY. Happy birthday, Papa.

THE DON. Baby, you sing like a song bird. (*Suddenly grabs her hair and pulls it.*) But if you ever go to another audition I'm gonna rip out you vocal chords one by one.

(*The DON turns and faces Valaria. HE is surprised to see her there. VALARIA just smiles wickedly. The encounter is brief and goes unnoticed by all.*)

CORRITA. Happy birthday, darling.

THE DON. (*Gives her a raspberry.*) That's what I think ofa you. (*THE DON heads for the chair behind his desk.*)

CORRITA. (*Trying.*) Would you like to open your presents now?

THE DON. I don't need no presents. I got the best present this morning. Nick the Fish and I came to a decision. Connie gonna marry Benito Scarelli, the hunchback who was over here last New Year's Eve.

CONNIE. That's it, stick the .
slowly. Torture me, Papa. Go on. Rip ᴗ
hang it out to dry. But I'll get even. (*CONNIᴸ*
the study steps and turns back.) And just for thᴗ
that's the worse Marlon Brando impression I ever hearᴅ.

THE DON. (*Growls.*) Grrrrrrrrrrrrrrrr!!!!!

(*CONNIE exits slamming study door.*)

ROBERTO. Papa, you wanna hear the poem I wrote for
you?

CORRITA. What's a matter for you. I said no!

(*The DON grabs Roberto by the face/chin.*)

ROBERTO. I wrote it especially for today.
THE DON. Yeah?
ROBERTO. Yeah! I wrote it especially for you?
THE DON. Yeah?
ROBERTO. Can I read it?

(*The DON slowly lowers Roberto's face into his birthday
cake. ROBERTO helplessly watches the cake get closer
and closer. HIS eyes bug-out and HE stifles a cry. When
the DON releases ROBERTO, his face is covered with
cake. HE stands and takes off his glasses. Humiliated,
HE exits sobbing.*)

THE DON. That felta good.
CORRITA. Why do you torture the boy?
THE DON. Don Giovani shouldn't have a son like that.
The Don is a definition of a great man.

CORRITA. And that's another thing. I'ma sick of this Don thing. The Don this and the Don that. Hey, big shot, your name is Donald. Donald, like the duck. Quack, quack. You're Donald Giovani. You thinka you ina the movies or something with diz the Don crap.

(BABY breaks into her "I say. I say. I say," etc. song. The DON raises a hand to strike Corrita, but doesn't. Instead the DON and CORRITA growl at each other.)

THE DON. Grrrrrrrrr.
CORRITA. Grrrrrrrr.

BLACKOUT

End of Scene 1

ACT I

Scene 2

AT RISE: During the BLACKOUT we hear three GUNSHOTS. A week has past since the Don's birthday. Wearing a leopard print hat and coat CONNIE frantically paces back and forth praying. SHE is chain-smoking and constantly going to the secret panel checking to see if Rocky is there. Finally, SHE sits on the sofa mumbling to herself. The set is in dark shadows. Slowly, the secret panel in the STAGE LEFT bookcase opens. A HAND appears pointing a gun. At

*first CONNIE doesn't see this, but when SHE does
SHE goes into action and crawls to the bookshelf.
Quickly, SHE pulls the INTRUDER in and karate
chops him, then flips him.*

CONNIE. What the hell is your problem, Rocky?

*(The INTRUDER stands. It's ROBERTO—frightened and
holding a white ski-mask.)*

ROBERTO. Connie it's me, ROBERTO. Don't hit me!
Don't hit me.

CONNIE. You? What the hell were you doing here?

ROBERTO. I was in there ... uh ... I was ... uh ...
reading some poetry.

CONNIE. With a gun?

ROBERTO. It was very volatile poetry.

CONNIE. *(Picking up the gun.)* Where'd you get the
gun?

ROBERTO. It's Papa's.

CONNIE. How do you know about the secret
passageway?

ROBERTO. When I was a kid Papa used to lock me in
the tunnels when he was mad at me.

CONNIE. What's that in your hand?

ROBERTO. My hat. What is this, Connie, twenty
questions?

CONNIE. *(Dead serious.)* I don't like pistols pointed in
my puss. Face

ROBERTO. I didn't know you was in here. I was just
playing with the gun. I came back to return it to Papa's

desk. (*Takes pistol and puts it back into the desk.*) What are *you* doing here?

CORRITA. (*Offstage.*) Don, we gotta talk.

(*CONNIE opens secret panel and shoves ROBERTO in it and follows him closing the panel behind her. The study door opens. THE DON and CORRITA enter. BABY follows.*)

THE DON. I'ma busy.
BABY. Please, Papa. It's real important.

(*THE DON goes to his desk and buries his head in papers.*)

CORRITA. It's not every day something like this happens in our family.
THE DON. It's about Baby?
CORRITA. Yes.
THE DON. I don't ask you questions about my business. Handle it, Corrita.

(*CORRITA and BABY smile, turn around, and cross to the stairs and up them.*)

THE DON. Hey, Corrita! Wait a minute.
CORRITA. I didn't think it'd be that easy.
THE DON. (*Suspicious.*) I gotta bad feeling I ain't gonna like whatever this is about.

(*From the foot of the study steps BABY runs to the Don's desk and leaps onto it crawling to her PAPA, who moves back in horror.*)

BABY. Oh, please say yes, Papa. Please say yes. I begggggggg you. It's the most important thing that's ever happened to me ever. I'll just die if you say no and I really mean I'll die. Like, I'll kill myself. And my death will be on your hands. So, please say yes and let me LIVE!!!!!

THE DON. Well, this isa easy. (*Gets into Baby's face.*) NO!

BABY. AGHHHHHHHHHHH!!!! (*BABY rolls off desk and plops on floor sobbing.*)

CORRITA. NO? You ain't even heard what she wants to ask you. How canna you say no?

THE DON. I put my tongue behinda my upper dentures and go NNNN making an OOOO with mya lips. NO! It's real simple.

CORRITA. This isa your daughter, Baby Theresa Giovani. She'a thinking, feeling caring person who has dreams. We all got dreams and we all gotta follow our heart, Don Giovani. Baby here wants to be a great singer. A famous singer. She gotta start somewheres ...

THE DON. Like where?

CORRITA. She got'a this small role in a musical offa Broadway.

BABY. Oh, please, Papa. Let me do it. Please, Papa with spumone and a cherry on top.

THE DON. (*Uncharacteristically smiling.*) They hired you? (*The DON seems to have a change of heart.*)

BABY. Yes, Papa.

CORRITA. It's a small role, Don, but, hey it's a role. Right?

THE DON. (*Happy.*) Right. Good for you, Baby. Good. When you auditioned for this play?

(CORRITA is smiling and nodding. SHE is pleased with this success.)

BABY. *(Smiling.)* It was about a month ago. I sung the hymn of the Battle of the Republic ... in I-talian.

THE DON. You didn't?

CORRITA. *(Smiling and nodding.)* She did.

BABY. I wore a backless black sequin evening gown ... with a red plume hat ... and canary yellow shoes.

THE DON. *(Smiling and laughing.)* You didn't?

CORRITA. *(Disapproving.)* She did.

BABY. I've been in rehearsal for three weeks now. You know dancing, singing lessons, costume fittings and stuff like that. I'm so exhausted at the end of the day, but I love it.

THE DON. What's the name of this play?

BABY. *Beat me, Beat me, Harder, Harder.*

THE DON. *(Laughing.)* It isn't?

CORRITA. *(Laughing and nodding.)* It is.

BABY. I play a pregnant nun.

(CORRITA makes an "Uh-oh" face.)

THE DON. *(Smiling.)* So, against my wishes you got yourself dressed up like a Third Avenue whore ... *(Anger building.)* ... and auditioned for a dirty musical in which you play a nun who got in the family way! *(To Corrita.)* WHAT KIND OF KIDS YOU RAISING, CORRITA? *(To Baby.)* NO!!! GET OUTTA HERE AND GO TO CHURCH so you can pray for forgiveness. Sixty-five

"Hail Marys" and twenty "Our Father Who START witha Heaven" gotta do you some good.

BABY. I hate you. I hate you.

THE DON. Just remember I'm the one who keeps you in black dresses and rosary beads, Baby. Now, get out of here!!!!!!!

BABY. I wish you were dead!!!!!!!! (*BABY runs out of the study screaming, sobbing and crying.*)

CORRITA. Why, Don Giovani? Why?

THE DON. (*Sarcastic.*) Beat me, Beat me, Harder, Harder.

CORRITA. (*Raising her hand in the air to the Don.*) I'd like to.

THE DON. What kind of a musical is that?

CORRITA. Everybody gotta start somewhere. Look, even Frank Sinatra had start on the bottom.

THE DON. (*Returning to his desk.*) Donna youa take a Sinatra's name ina vain!

CORRITA. (*Tries a new tactic. SHE goes around the Don and begins massaging his shoulders.*) Donnie? Donnie Giovani, my meatball man. Baby is such a good singer and I know youa so proud of her. Times change, Don. Donna you wanna the whole city to know justa how gooda she sings?

THE DON. Mobster's daughters donna have singing careers. They marry second-rate hoods—like Connie's gonna do

CORRITA. Says a who?

THE DON. Says a me. That's who.

CORRITA. Connie don't wanna marry anybody she don't love.

THE DON. (*Grabs chest dramatically.*) Look, you giving me a pain right here. Connie gonna marry who I tell her to marry and it gonna be One-eyed Joe Provolone. He's coming here today to make final arrangements.

CORRITA. She's a thirty-three years old. Donna you think she can make-a up her own mind?

THE DON. And who-a you want to let her marry ... Rocky Studds Malone?

CORRITA. (*Knows about it and reacts accordingly.*) Okay. Connie marry who-a you say. But the Baby ... let Baby be in this show 'cause it means so much to her and you love her so much.

THE DON. Mobster's daughters don't have singing careers.

GINO. (*Enters.*) Papa. I got One-eyed Joe Provolone out here.

THE DON. Bringa him in, Gino.

(*GINO exits.*)

THE DON. (*To Corrita.*) You! Get outta here and make-a me dinner!

CORRITA. You making a big mistake, Don!

THE DON. I know. We should go to a restaurant. Your cooking stinks.

CORRITA. (*Growls to Don.*) Grrrrrrr!!

THE DON. (*"Right back at cha."*) Grrrrrrrr!!

(*CORRITA exits as GINO ushers in ONE-EYED JOE. The man is a fat, nervous, slouching fellow with shifty eyes and a somewhat feminine aura about him. Somewhere between 50 and 60 with a squeaky heavy*

Italian accent. He is the most important part of the
Death of a Don. *He is the key to this whole story. JOE*
is really ROCKY in fat padding, heavy make-up and
wig. A big nose and a scar on the forehead add to the
illusion. Also HE has a pirate's patch on his right eye.
HE walks hunched over giving the impression that he
is shorter than he really is. Distinguishing these
characters is the key to fooling the audience and
bringing this mystery/comedy to a roaring success.
ONE-EYED JOE nervously walks down the steps of the
study looking from side to side at these new
surroundings. HE semi-runs to the Don and kisses his
ring.)

ONE-EYED JOE. Don Giovani, I wisha only the besta
for you family and yourself.

THE DON. One-eyed Joe, have a seat. Make-a yourself
comfortable.

(GINO stands guard at the head of the stairs. JOE sits in a
reception chair.)

ONE-EYED JOE. It's a honor to help you, Don
Giovani.

THE DON. I know.

ONE-EYED JOE. It's a honor to be asked to your home
too.

THE DON. *(Nodding and smiling.)* I know.

ONE-EYED JOE. Is just an honor to be in this chair.

THE DON. *(Loud; interrupting.)* It's gonna be an honor
for me to punch you in the faze if you donna shutta up
with this honor crap.

ONE-EYED JOE. I'm so sorry, Don Giovani. I no wanna make you upset.

THE DON. Did Nick the Fish tell you whata I want from you?

ONE-EYED JOE. He no say anything before Rocky Studds Malone gang rubba him out. I so upset. I no eat for a whole day.

THE DON. Nick was a good man. Why anybody would kill him, even the Malone gang, is a mystery to me. As you know, Nick was not a member of our family, though he was a good friend. His death was senseless, but we're gonna avenge him by killing Rocky Studds Malone once and for all. (*Pause.*) One-eyed Joe, I got a dangerous mission for you.

ONE-EYED JOE. (*Frightened.*) You wanna me to kill Rocky Studds Malone?

THE DON. No.

ONE-EYED JOE. (*In shock.*) More dangerous than killing Rocky Studds Malone?

THE DON. I'm gonna make you an offer you can't refuse.

(*A little Italian MUSIC begins here. The DON, GINO and JOE look up suspiciously.*)

GINO. (*After several beats.*) Mama's playing some records upstairs.

THE DON. Joe, I wanna you to marry my daughter.

ONE-EYED JOE. The little fat one that sings.

THE DON. No. My oldest daughter, Connie Elaine.

ONE-EYED JOE. (*Mortal terror.*) CONNIE! Connie who bit off Rossicone's ear last Christmas?

(THE DON smiles and nods.)

ONE-EYED JOE. *(Fear; high pitched.)* Connie?

THE DON. You are the second man who has been offered this opportunity.

ONE-EYED JOE. What happened to the first?

THE DON. He's no longer ... among us.

ONE-EYED JOE. Am I such a lucky son-of-a-bitch or what. I ... I ... I'd love to marry her, Don Giovani.

THE DON. Any man would.

ONE-EYED JOE. I will ... uh ... treat like ... like ... she was my own ... uh ... daughter. Yeah. Like she was my own daughter.

(The study door slams open. CONNIE in her leopard outfit charges in. She pushes GINO down the steps.)

CONNIE. YOU BASTARDS! I ain't cattle. You can't buy and sell me.

THE DON. *(Insulted, HE stands up screaming.)* You gonna marry who I tell you to marry or you ain't ever gonna see the insides of Bloomingdale's again.

CONNIE. And who made you God?

THE DON. I gave birth to you. I can do anything I want. You got that?

ONE-EYED JOE. If she donna wanna ... I ...

THE DON. *(Interrupting.)* Sit down. *(To Connie.)* You shut-up. *(Smiling.)* Meet your future husband. One-eyed Joe Provolone, this is the bride.

CONNIE. Cheese? You're making me marry someone whose last name is cheese and who smells like fish?!!

THE DON. Provolone isa a good Italian name. And the fish market's a good racket. You'll live in luxury. (*To Joe.*) Won't she?

JOE. Oh, yes. Of course she will. Anything you wanna.

THE DON. Joe, tell Connie a little bit about yourself.

(ONE-EYED JOE steps closer to Connie and smiles like a nerd.)

CONNIE. Don't smile at me.

ONE-EYED JOE. Well, I'm a Libra with Leo rising and I play miniature golf every Saturday night. I like watching the TV and my hobby is a collecting Ann-Margret memorabilia. I am employed to collect protection money from the wharf.

CONNIE. (*To the Don.*) You gotta be kidding me? You want me to marry this?

ONE-EYED JOE. I canna make you very happy, Connie. It'll be a simple arrangement. You cook, clean, entertain my business associates, be a hostess and raise babies.

CONNIE. (*Rage.*) Babies????

ONE-EYED JOE. Lot'a babies.

CONNIE. That's it!

THE DON. (*Warning.*) CONNIE.

CONNIE. Shut up, old man.

(CONNIE pushes the DON into his desk and pushes ONE-EYED JOE into his chair.)

CONNIE. (*To Joe.*) If you marry me I'll make your life a living HELL! Hell, you hear?

ONE-EYED JOE. I hear! I hear!

CONNIE. (*Pulls JOE up by his ear.*) I'll give new meaning to fear. You'll go to bed every night wondering if that's the night I've chosen to stick the knife in your heart. (*CONNIE pushes JOE to the floor.*)

THE DON. (*Screaming.*) Gino! Gino! Gino getta her outta here!

(*GINO comes from behind and picking her up as SHE begins screaming and throwing her arms everywhere.*)

CONNIE. No sex! I don't cook and I don't clean!

THE DON. (*"Right back at you."*) Big deal! That's the way I've been living for the last twenty years.

CONNIE. And as for you ... (*CONNIE tries to get away from Gino in an attempt to get her hands on the Don.*) ... you son-of-a-bitch. Stay away from dark alleys 'cause I'm gonna kill you. Do you hear me?

THE DON. The whole world hears you and your big mouth.

CONNIE. I'm gonna knife you, shoot you, bash you and then throw your battered body in a vat of cement and toss you in the goddamn river.

THE DON. Get the blushing bride outta here.

(*CONNIE screams. GINO removes her from the study.*)

CONNIE. (*Fades as she is taken from room.*) After I kill Papa I'm gonna come back for you—you one-eyed creep and I gonna boil you in oil and then I'm gonna get you, GINO, for helping ...

(The DON smooths his hair back and smiles to Joe as HE helps him up from the floor.)

THE DON. Look at it this way, Joe. You ain't ever gonna be bored. *(The DON sits at his desk.)* So? Are you still interested in treating my daughter as if she was your own?

ONE-EYED JOE. Do I gotta any choice?

THE DON. *(Flashes a big smile indicating "no.")* She likes you. I can tell. Anyway, does it matter? The wedding invitations already went out. *(Loud and commanding.)* NOW GET OUTTA MY FAZE.

(JOE nervously runs up the stairs.)

GINO. *(Enters.)* Hey, Pop. Boy, is Connie mad at us. I had to lock her in a closet. *(Sits in reception chair.)* So are you ready?

THE DON. For what?

GINO. The 976 numbers. You said we could talk today. I gave you a proposal packet, video, fiscal graph and a demographics report.

THE DON. Who do you think I am? The Chairman of the Board of A.T.T & P? If you got something on your mind just level with me, Gino.

GINO. My report clearly shows that we can make a bundle. Implementing computer technology allows a substantial reduction in employees. We save on insurance, headaches and government tax. That alone makes the entire package more appealing to a corporation such as ours. Little to no customer contact compounded with the low profile this type of service maintains is perfect for us to make a killing. Financially speaking, of course.

THE DON. (*Totally lost.*) What the HELL are you talking about?

GINO. If you had read the proposal you'd understand.

THE DON. I sent you to college so I wouldn't have to read.

GINO. Papa, just give me the dollar go ahead. It's a great idea.

THE DON. It's a dumb idea.

GINO. How can you say that when the facts and figures prove how much the family can make.

THE DON. You sick. I know what this 976 crap is all about. I got eyes. I watch late night TV. Smut. 976-Come jump my bones. That's what this is all about.

GINO. Why don't you like any of my ideas?

THE DON. 'Cause they stink! You wanna bring heavy breathing and dirty phone calls to the mob. Who do you think I am? *HUGE HEFINER?????*

GINO. But the money we can make ...

THE DON. (*Interrupting.*) If I don't get any sex I don't see why anybody else should!!!!!

GINO. (*The father and son battle is on.*) BULL! Maybe you don't like my idea for another reason.

THE DON. I don't like your idea 'cause it's stupid!!!!!

GINO. Maybe I'm never taken serious 'cause I ain't from the loins of your precious wife.

THE DON. What are you talking about?

GINO. Don't be coy with me, old man. Everybody in the family knows. It's not as if your wife goes out of her way to hide it.

THE DON. Who put this idea into your fat head?

GINO. Your wife.

THE DON. Get out of here.

GINO. Who was my real mother, Papa?

THE DON. You're crazy.

GINO. And you're a bad liar. If you were dead and I had control over this business we'd all be rich.

THE DON. If I was dead I'd be rolling over in my grave.

GINO. Some day you're gonna regret not listening to me.

THE DON. And someday they're gonna find Jimmy Hoffa's body. I'll take my chances.

GINO. The least you can do is tell him who my real mother is.

THE DON. Get the hell outta here!

GINO. A show girl? A maid? Who was my mother, Papa? An ex-mistress or some two bit whore from ...

THE DON. (*Slaps Gino across the face.*) Sharper than a serpent's tooth is an ungrateful child. You SON-OF-A-BITCH!

(*ROBERTO enters with a broken tennis racket. HE has a black eye and looks roughed up. THE DON and GINO continue to stare at each other with hate.*)

ROBERTO. I'm having a very bad day, Papa.

(Still staring at the Don, GINO backs up slowly, but says nothing.)

ROBERTO. *(To Gino.)* Hi, Gino. You're not gonna believe what ... hey, where you going?

(GINO exits and slams door. THE DON ignores ROBERTO and continues working at desk.)

ROBERTO. Papa, I got bad news. Some men beat me up and told me to give you a message.

THE DON. God in heaven. Where did your mother go wrong.

ROBERTO. *(Walks over to the Don.)* These men told to me to ...

(ROBERTO grabs The Don's head and kisses him. The DON becomes hysterical.)

THE DON. What is this thing with kissing me? Don't ever kiss me! Don't ever touch me!

ROBERTO. Don't you get it, Papa?

THE DON. What the hell are you talking about?

BABY. *(Enters. Sarcastic.)* There's no other place for me to do my daily scales, Papa and I know how you LOVE to hear me sing. *(BABY begins singing the scales.)*

ROBERTO. Papa, it was the Malone gang that beat me up.

THE DON. *(A little overwhelmed.)* What? *(To Baby.)* Please, Baby, not here.

ROBERTO. *(Screaming.)* That was the kiss of death, Papa.

*(Suddenly the study doors open and CONNIE rushes in.
    Not far behind is CORRITA.)*

CONNIE. *(To the Don.)* You son-of-a-bitch!!?

THE DON. Leave your grandmother out of this!

CORRITA. Connie, please I beg you.

THE DON. *(To Connie.)* What the hell do you want?

CONNIE. Murderer!

ROBERTO. Would you listen to me, Papa.

CORRITA. This ain't a good time, Connie.

CONNIE. You killed Rocky Studds Malone. He's dead!!!

ROBERTO. That's what I'm trying to tell you, Papa. The Malone gang found out you killed Rocky Studds Malone and now they've declared war on us Giovanis.

THE DON. Baby—SHUT UP!!!

GINO. *(Appears at the door screaming.)* I want some respect in this family!

THE DON. I'll give you respect right across your faze. *(To Connie.)* Connie what is going on? Why do you care about ...

CONNIE. Rocky Studds Malone was my dark knight in shining Brooks Brothers pin-striped. You just killed the best piece of ass I ever had.

CORRITA. Oh, God in heaven!

(Silence.)

THE DON. You disgrace me. All of youse. I ain't got no family.

(A melee ensues, EVERYONE speaks simultaneously. CONNIE and CORRITA start yelling at each other. BABY begins singing scales again. GINO comes down the stairs yelling at Corrita. THE DON hits Roberto across the head as HE crosses to stairs. CORRITA yells at Connie and Gino. The DON shakes his head and walks up the study steps.)

CONNIE. My own father's a glob of spit. How could you let him Mama? *(Etc.)*

CORRITA. Forty years I haven't been able to do anything, Connie. *(Etc.)*

GINO. Who's my real mother? I demand to know. I know my rights ... *(Etc.)*

CORRITA. I'm your mother and I got the stretch marks to prove it ... *(Etc.)*

ROBERTO. I was nearly murdered in broad daylight and he hits me... *(Etc.)*

CONNIE. I ain't marrying the fish man. I refuse. I'll kill him first ....

GINO. Nobody listens to my ideas and I'm sick of it ... *(Etc.)*

CORRITA. You try living with him for forty years ... go on, I dare you!!!

(BABY continues singing scales. At the top of the study stairs THE DON turns around and looks at them. HE exits. The rest of the FAMILY continues yelling at each other as the LIGHTS FADE and we hear:)

THE DON. *(Voice over.)* This family's gonna be the death of me yet!

End of Scene 2

ACT I

Scene 3

AT RISE: Two weeks have passed. VALARIA, dressed up, but cheaply, nervously paces the study clutching a pink handbag. After five beats the DON enters wearing a tuxedo clutching an envelope. VALARIA smiles sitting in a reception chair. HE sits behind his desk staring at her with hate. SHE leans over to grab the envelope and HE slaps her hand.

THE DON. Such a grabby woman.
VALARIA. (*Smiles.*) So I've been told.
THE DON. (*After a beat HE hands her envelope.*) Stay away from my son.

(VALARIA stands and puts the envelope in her handbag. BABY walks in, sees the scene, backs up and watches from behind the door with interest.)

VALARIA. You take care too. I wouldn't want ... anything ... happening to you.
CORRITA. (*Offstage. Sweetly.*) Donnie! Oh, Donnie. Where are you? We gonna take pictures.

(BABY withdraws her head. VALARIA turns toward the stairs.)

THE DON. You ain't going out that 'a way. This way.

(BABY pops her head in. THE DON pulls a book from the STAGE LEFT bookshelf and the secret panel pops open.)

CORRITA. *(Offstage.)* Baby! Whata ya doing there? Is Papa ina his study?

(THE DON pulls VALARIA and shoves her behind the secret panel closing it after her. CORRITA enters wearing a pink dress.)

CORRITA. *(To The Don.)* What the hell are ya doing in here? We got pictures to take. Hey maybe we take a few family snaps in here. I'm tired of taking pictures ina front of that ice sculpture of Caruso.
THE DON. Why'a you hire a photographer? We got Sophia taking polaroids of anything that moves.
CORRITA. I sent Baby to go find Connie and One-eyed Joe. We gonna take pictures in here.
THE DON. No, we ain't ...

(CORRITA takes THE DON by the hands and leads him to the sofa. ROBERTO enters and crosses to desk suspiciously.)

CORRITA. What you say don't matter. Today isa happy day. Today I do anything I want 'cause my first born got married today. Besides Sophia's so stupid she couldn't manage a picture of her thumb.

(CORRITA and THE DON sit.)

ROBERTO. Connie ain't your first born, Mama. Gino's two years older than ...

(MAMA closes her eyes letting the anger pass.)

THE DON. *(Interrupting.)* Shut-up! Since when do you know how to do math?

CORRITA. It was a beautiful wedding. But I wish Connie wouldn't keep calling One-Eyed Joe a Cyclops.

(CORRITA cuddles up to The Don. ROBERTO slowly opens The Don's desk drawer.)

CORRITA. Now that a Connie isa married why don't we take Roberto and the Baby and go to Disney World.

THE DON. No.

CORRITA. Why?

THE DON. 'Cause I said so.

(ROBERTO slowly removes the gun from the Don's drawer. CORRITA stands up and gets in front of the Don blocking his view to Roberto.)

CORRITA. I wanna go ona vacation and I wanna go to Disney World.

(ROBERTO stuffs the gun into his jacket.)

THE DON. I donna wanna.

CORRITA. And I wanna.

THE DON. Mobsters don't go to Disney World.

CORRITA. Says a who?

THE DON. Says a me that's a who.

CORRITA. And just where the hell do you get your information?

THE DON. What information? I make it up as I go along. It's easier that way.

CORRITA. Someday ... when you're dead ... I'm gonna get to do what I wanna do.

THE DON. No you ain't, 'cause I'm gonna come back and haunt you till you die, woman!

CORRITA. Grrrrrrrrrrrrrrrrrrrr.

THE DON. Grrrrrrrrrrrrrrrrrrrr.

(CONNIE appears at the study door. Her wedding dress is a white mini-skirt with too many bows on it. The veil is rigged to a high-fashion hat with plumbs sticking out. SHE's carrying her bouquet and a large, white handbag.)

CONNIE. I want a drink.

THE DON. Go to the outside bar like everyone else.

CONNIE. *(Enters and heads for the bar. SHE pours a drink.)* Whose bright idea was it to water down all the booze, Papa?

THE DON. You're married now. You don't need to drink.

CONNIE. I'm gonna get so drunk, I'm gonna forget we're family.

THE DON. Just don't forget whose bed you're sleeping in tonight.

CONNIE. A one-eyed mutant from fish town isn't very easy to forget. All I gotta do is take a whiff of him to remind me how much I hate you, Papa.

CORRITA. (*To Connie.*) That's enough, Connie.

(*BABY and GINO enter. CORRITA goes to Connie to calm her down. BABY joins them. THE DON crosses to his desk.*)

GINO. (*To the Don.*) Hey, Papa. Where you been? I been looking for you. I sent Valaria to the liquor store to get some real booze. The whiskey tastes like iced tea.

THE DON. That tramp is still here. (*To Roberto.*) Get outta my chair. This is my desk.

(*ROBERTO crosses to reception chairs and sits. THE DON watches Roberto's every move. HE is not listening to Gino.*)

GINO. Hey. She's my date, Papa. Lay off. You ain't exactly got the greatest taste in women either.

CORRITA. (*To Gino.*) Don't make me lose my temperature, big shot.

GINO. Look, Papa. I got Vinnie de Vinci outside. He wants to talk with you. He likes my 976 number idea. You gotta listen to him.

THE DON. (*Puts his elbows on his desk and rests his head in his hands as HE continues staring at Roberto.*) I ain't gotta do anything but avoid taxes and die.

ROBERTO. Well, you gotta go to the bathroom too.

THE DON. (*To Roberto.*) When a Gino was your age he already killed six people.

GINO. Papa, Vinnie says marriage is out. Telephone relationships are in.

ROBERTO. I couldn't kill anyone, Papa.

THE DON. No? Then how come you're killing me.

(GINO continues talking as THE DON belittles Roberto. ROBERTO remains terrified.)

GINO. This godfather image is strictly for Hollywood. Time moves on. You know the Malone gang is using computers.

THE DON. *(To Roberto.)* Past twenty-one and still a virgin. What kind of a son is that for The Don?

GINO. We can legalize the family business with this 976 craze.

THE DON. *(Leans over the desk and grabs Roberto by the collar. To Roberto.)* Why do you read those romance books? That ain't normal.

GINO. We can make a killing in the market, Papa. And just think our free enterprising notions ...

THE DON. *(To Roberto.)* Who ever thought I'd have a poet for a son?

ROBERTO. Why can't you accept me for the artist that I am?

GINO. ... will earn us tax breaks and a pat on the back from Uncle Sam.

THE DON. *(To Roberto.)* Get on your knees.

(THE DON shoves the crying ROBERTO to the floor and then slaps Gino.)

THE DON. *(To Gino.)* You ain't got an Uncle Sam.

*(CORRITA rushes to Roberto. GINO snarls at The Don
and crosses to bar. GINO pours himself a drink.)*

CORRITA. Can't you leave wella enough alone? Why
couldn't you just let him be for one day? *(To Roberto.)*
There ... there, Roberto. Papa, didn't mean it. He loves
you.

THE DON. This is your fault Corrita. He's from your
side of the family.

CORRITA. Half of those chromosomes were yours,
buddy boy.

CONNIE. Ain't this a hell of a wedding? *(Raises her
glass.)* A toast to the biggest cow pie east of the midwest,
my father.

CORRITA. Connie!

BABY. *(Overcome by emotion.)* I guess this is as good
as time as any to give Connie a special gift from me to my
big sister with love. *(BABY leans over and kisses Connie.)*

CONNIE. Watch my hair. Watch my hair.

CORRITA. *(To Connie.)* It looks fine. Listen to your
baby sister.

*(BABY clasps her hands together over her stomach and lifts
her head to the heavens.)*

CONNIE. *(Disgusted.)* You're gonna sing? That's my
present? A crummy song?

BABY. Not just any song. *(Begins singing.)*
I say. I say. I say.
Happy wedding, dear sis ...

CONNIE. (*Shoves her bouquet into Baby's face.*) Shut-up. You sound like a moose in labor.

BABY. (*Whining.*) A mooooosssseeeee??????

CONNIE. Somebody get me a drink.

(ROBERTO runs to the bar and begins making her a drink. ONE-EYED JOE enters wearing a tuxedo with a pink shirt.)

ONE-EYED JOE. (*Clapping his hands together happily.*) This is the happiest day of my life. I so happy I could cry.

CONNIE. I'll give you something to cry about. Get your one-eyed puss down here. We're takin' pictures.

ONE-EYED JOE. (*Comes down the stairs and crosses to Connie.*) Oh, Connie it's such a beautiful a day. Everything isa so beautiful. I am naturally delirious. I've had six drinks and still I no feel drunk.

(CONNIE turns to The Don and gives him a dirty look.)

ONE-EYED JOE. Connie. I'm gonna say a few things here now. In front of your family. Things I really feel. Connie, I'm gonna take good care of you. I'm gonna be the best husband you ever thought possible. And someday. Youa gonna look at me ... (*ONE-EYED JOE breaks into a wide smile.*)

CONNIE. Don't smile at me.

ONE-EYED JOE. (*A grave look.*) Youa gonna look at me and youa gonna say. Joe, I love you.

CONNIE. Now get this straight. There's only one man I'll ever love. (*CONNIE removes an 8 x 10 glossy of*

Rocky from her purse.) See him. That's Rocky Studds Malone. This is the man I will always love.

THE DON. He's a dead. So, ~~unless you're a velcrophilic~~ ... (*Pause.*) ... you might as well enjoy fat man over here.

ONE-EYED JOE. Love me, Connie.

(*JOE puts his arms around CONNIE who in turns knees him in the groin. CONNIE puts Rocky's picture back into her purse.*)

CONNIE. Touch me again, Cyclops, and I'll braid the family jewels 'til you're singing soprano next to the moose over there.

THE DON. It's gonna be a hellva honeymoona night.

CORRITA. Pictures. Pictures. Okay, Don, come on over here we're gonna take pictures. The bride and the gr ... (*Hesitates.*) One-Eyed Joe at the foot of the stairs. The bride on the left and the ... (*Hesitates—moves Connie into place.*) One-Eyed Joe on the right. (*To Connie.*) My God, Connie, you smell like day-old fish.

CONNIE. (*Slow turn to Joe.*) I wonder why?

(*CONNIE and JOE cross to CENTER STAGE. CORRITA situates them at the foot of the stairs.*)

CORRITA. Right, a here. Roberto stand next to you brother-in-law, Baby next to Connie. Don, you get next to Roberto at the end.

(*EVERYONE arranges themselves accordingly. CONNIE and BABY growl at each other. THE DON growls at*

ROBERTO, who cowers. CORRITA steps back and views the set up.)

CORRITA. No. That ain't right. Don, go stand next to Baby.

(THE DON does but not without making faces.)

CORRITA. No. Something ain't right. Don, go stand next to Roberto again.
THE DON. Don't push me, Corrita.

(THE DON crosses to Roberto.)

CORRITA. Something's still not right and I can't ...

(GINO, standing by the bar, coughs loudly.)

CORRITA. ... figure out what ...

(GINO coughs.)

CORRITA. ... is no good. *(Knowingly turns to Gino.)* Ohhhhhhhhhhhhhhh. Gino. I seemed to have forgot you. Go stand next to Baby.

(GINO gets into place.)

CORRITA. Perfect. Well, as perfect as this family can get.
CORRITA. *(Stands next to Gino.)* Now everybody smile.

(All at once EVERYONE breaks into a fake smile. From left to right we have CORRITA, GINO, BABY, CONNIE, ONE-EYED JOE, ROBERTO and THE DON. THEY stand perfectly still for three beats. Then ONE-EYED JOE closes his eyes and accidently bumps into Connie. CONNIE elbows Joe in the gut. JOE bumps into ROBERTO who pushes JOE into CONNIE. CONNIE, in turn, bumps into BABY and suddenly ALL HELL BREAKS LOOSE. FAMILY MEMBERS begin improvising, pushing and yelling at each other simultaneously. For example CORRITA begins hitting Gino and yelling at him.)

CORRITA. *(To Gino.)* You're so stupid. You never listen. You upset the whole family. You and that tramp. *(Etc.)*

GINO. *(To Corrita.)* Don't think I don't know your little secret. I know you hate me, I always have, but what you don't know is I hate you right back. *(Etc.)*

THE DON. *(Strikes Roberto repeatedly, To Roberto.)* On your knees. You're nothing but a boil on my butt. I ain't ever seen such a sorry sight in all my life. Look at you. You coward. Why are you on your knees? *(Etc.)*

ROBERTO. *(Crying.)* Why don't you just kill me? Go ahead. Kill me. Put me out of your misery. I just want to write poems. Poems. That's all. Is that so much to ask? *(Etc.)*

(BABY and CONNIE fight—CONNIE hits Baby with her bouquet. ONE-EYED JOE is between them.)

CONNIE. (*To Baby.*) I don't ever want to hear you sing again. You stink. You're tone deaf and fat. (*Etc.*)

BABY. (*To Connie.*) You just think the world of yourself, don't cha. Well, there are some people in this family who would rather have a woman with talent than a cheap hussy like you. (*Etc.*)

(*ONE-EYED JOE is blown away by his new family and looks at everyone in awe.*
After three or four beats this melee comes to a close with...)

THE DON. (*At the top of his lungs.*) WILL YOUSE ALL SHUT-UP. WE'RE TAKING PICTURES HERE!!!

(*Quickly EVERYONE gets back into place, a beat later THEY resume the fake smile. Three beats pass.*)

THE DON. WHERE THE HELL IS THE PHOTOGRAPHER!!!!

CORRITA. (*Horrified.*) Oh, my God. I forgot to get the photographer. Everybody wait one second.

(*The FAMILY disperses. ROBERTO quickly exits up the staircase and through the study door. CONNIE goes to the bar. ONE-EYED JOE also exits.*)

CORRITA. (*Turns to Baby.*) Go find that no good photographer. (*Calling to Roberto.*) Roberto come back here.

(*BABY exits. CONNIE takes a vodka bottle. GINO goes up the stairs.*)

CORRITA. Gino!

GINO. Valaria should be back by now.

CORRITA. You stay. The photographer will be here soon. Connie where are you going?

CONNIE. (*Crosses to the stairs.*) I'm gonna go mingle with my guests. Any objections?

CORRITA. (*Screaming.*) That's it.

(*EVERYONE freezes.*)

CORRITA. Nobody listen to me. I don't exist. I don't need wedding photos of my daughter's wedding. Everybody disobey me!

(*A beat later GINO and CONNIE exit. CORRITA watches in horror as they defy her. With an evil expression SHE turns on The Don.*)

CORRITA. You were the one who wanted kids. NOT ME!

THE DON. And you raised them to be all screwed up.

CORRITA. Grrrrrrrrrrrrrrrrrrrrrrr.

THE DON. Grrrrrrrrrrrrrrrrrrrrrrr.

(*CORRITA exits. THE DON turns off the banker's light and stands.*)

THE DON. For forty years I've struggled to give diz family a good home, food on the table, clothes on their backs and the dignity of my name. For forty years I think of nothing but work so I can give them everything they should have. *(The DON crosses to the bar.)* And what do I get ina return?

(The secret panel opens and a gloved HAND holding a gun arm emerges. Three SHOTS are fired into THE DON's back and HE falls to the floor. The ARM disappears and the panel closes. A beat later BABY enters.)

BABY. Papa? Papa?

(SHE steps down the stairs slowly and creeps toward the body. BABY looks at it close enough to know what has happened to the Don. Stifling her scream SHE runs back up and exits. Suggest the following be recorded as MUSIC builds.)

BABY. *(Offstage.)* Mama! Mama! Papa's dead. Papa's dead.

MAMA. *(Offstage.)* Again?

BABY. *(Offstage.)* He's really dead, Mama.

MAMA. *(Offstage.)* He's justa pulling your leg. He's teasing again.

BABY. *(Offstage.)* I saw him. He got bullets through his heart.

MAMA *(Offstage.)* See. There you are. He's faking again. Your papa doesn't have a heart.

*(Italian MUSIC up.
LIGHTS Fade.)*

End of Act I

ACT II

Scene 1

AT RISE: Minutes have passed. CORRITA rushes in followed by BABY and GINO who move the body together and place it on the sofa. GINO looks at the body closely. CORRITA stays CENTER STAGE waiting for Gino's assessment.

CORRITA. So? Don't keep me ina suspense, Gino. Is he or ain't he?

GINO. He's dead all right. Nice, clean break of the skin. Three slugs lodged in the main artery of the heart. He didn't know what the hell hit him. I'd say it was done with a .22 at close range. Nice job, really. I take my hat off to the killer.

(BABY gives Gino a dirty look. CORRITA runs to the body wailing.)

CORRITA. *(Kneeling next to the body.)* Oh, God in heaven, not my Donnie Giovani. My lamb. The love of my life. The man I've shared everything with. He wasn't a bad man. Sure, he killed people, but he never killed nobody on a Sunday.

(CONNIE appears at the study. BABY kneels next to Corrita and sobs.)

CORRITA. Did I ever tell you the time he knocked over a toy store once justa so I could have a mink coat? He wasa the salt of the earth even ifa my mother hated him. I canna believe he's gone.

CONNIE. (*To Gino.*) We're sure this time?

GINO. He ain't breathing.

CONNIE. That doesn't mean he's dead.

GINO. I can't feel a pulse.

(CORRITA wails.)

CONNIE. (*Looking around.*) Don't you think we ought to hit him with something heavy just to be on the safe side?

GINO. Connie, the man has three bullet holes in him.

(CORRITA wails louder.)

CONNIE. He's dead.

GINO. (*Snap.*) He's dead.

(BABY and CORRITA wail.)

CONNIE. (*Building.*) Mama! MAMA! I want a divorce. I want a divorce right now.

CORRITA. (*Wailing.*) My Don Giovani. My little meatball man.

CONNIE. (*To Gino.*) Gino. In light of this sudden event I would like you to go upstairs and get rid of those wedding guests. And tell the Cyclops I'd like a word with his fish face. Oh, and Gino, make sure the presents stay right where they are.

GINO. (*Angry.*) Don't think you're gonna start giving me orders, Connie.

CORRITA. (*Wailing.*) I canna believe he's a dead.

ROBERTO. (*Appears at the study door.*) What's going on?

CONNIE. The old man bought the farm.

CORRITA. (*Warning.*) Connie.

ROBERTO. Dead? Papa is dead. (*ROBERTO falls to his knees, drops his head and sobs. After two beats HE rises and recites with dramatic flair.*)

The angel of death has run and dear dad has gone to
    kingdom come.

It's too late to amend his ways, now, here at the end of his
    days.

I am sad, like a rose, but it is I who knows

the many times he was cruel.

The days and nights he called me fool.

How many times sent to bed without being fed

Yet I'm alive and he is dead.

(*Pause.*)

The walls melt around my prison cell.

Still, it's sad to think of the Don in hell.

(*BABY begins frantically applauding. ROBERTO becomes emotional and joins CORRITA and BABY near the body.*)

GINO. (*To Roberto.*) You are one mentally disturbed, S. O. B.

ONE-EYED JOE. (*Appears at the study door.*) There you all are. (*Coming down the stairs.*) The photographer wants us all by the fog machine. (*Crossing to sofa.*) What isa with the Don, he no look so good.

CORRITA. He's dead. Dead as a fish.

(*Frightened at seeing the dead Don, ONE-EYED JOE jumps back, turns and comes face to face with Connie.*)

CONNIE. You better be scared, dough boy 'cause your days are numbered. I'm on the phone to my lawyers as we speak. And believe me squid face we're gonna drain you dry. Half your house. A new car. Half the money in your bank and then alimony 'till you're broke. The Don is dead and I'm taking control.

(*GINO's face hits the ground. Anger takes over. Slowly HE turns toward his sister.*)

GINO. (*Loudly.*) Control of what?

CONNIE. (*To Gino.*) You don't think Papa left the business to you, do you?

GINO. (*Laughing.*) Don't think any of the family hoods are gonna listen to a self-appointed bimbo.

CONNIE. They ain't got no choice.

GINO. You ain't a Giovani no more. Youse a Provolone.

CONNIE. Temporarily.

GINO. I ain't decided that yet.

CONNIE. You ain't decided? You! Mister 976? You don't want to continue the traditions of our family. You want to turn us into a ~~horny~~ *raunchy* telephone franchise.

(GINO and CONNIE get closer and closer as they argue.)

GINO. Just 'cause you write out checks and balance the books don't mean you know anything about our business, Connie.

CONNIE. I know just as much as you, Gino.

GINO. I'm the oldest, I got the best college degree money could buy and on top of all that I'm the only male in this family.

ROBERTO. *(To Gino.)* Excuse me? What am I?

GINO. A poet.

CONNIE. Papa liked me best.

GINO. If he liked you so much how come he made you marry the one-eyed creep from hell? *(To One-Eyed Joe.)* Nothing personal, Joe.

(CONNIE and GINO begin a sibling war of yelling emotions and pent-up anger.)

CONNIE. At least I'm Giovani true and true which is more than I can say for you, half breed.

GINO. What the hell is that suppose to mean?

CONNIE. At least I know who my mother is.

GINO. Who my mother is or was doesn't change my father's will. I'm the only one in this family who's responsible for the future of the Giovani name. *(Quickly to Roberto.)* And I don't want any comment outta you, pansy!

CONNIE. I'll adopt. Connie Giovani and her daughters will rule this gang with an iron fist.

GINO. I'll give you a fist.

CONNIE. I'm gonna become the head of this family whether you like it or not.

GINO. I can just see Rat Chow Charlie and Toehead taking orders from a broad.

CONNIE. They'll listen to me if they know what's good for 'em.

GINO. Seems Papa's death fits right into your plans for the future. You get rid of your husband on your wedding day and take control of the family business. (*Walks to Connie.*) How convenient Papa took three slugs today. Seeing how it wasn't a wedding gift from Papa I guess I gotta think the old man was murdered.

CORRITA. (*Shriek.*) MURDERED??????!!!

BABY.. (*Crying.*) AGGGGGGGGHHHHHHH!!!!!

GINO. There he is. (*Gets into Connie's face.*) And here's Connie talking about being queen of the mafia. Sounds suspicious to me.

CONNIE. Get your puss outta my face before I do a Picasso number on it.

GINO. Hitting too close to home, Connie?

CONNIE. Grrrrrrrrrrrrrrrrrrrrrrrrr.

GINO. You hated him, didn't you?

CONNIE. Why I ought to ...

(*GINO and CONNIE attack each other. GINO goes for her throat and CONNIE tries to kick him in the groin. ROBERTO hits Gino. BABY hits Connie. JOE stands back frightened. THEY all improvise.*)

GINO. Just cause youse my sister, don't mean I can't knock you around. (*Etc.*)

CONNIE. You ain't smart enough to run a marathon let alone run a business. (*Etc.*)

BABY. Get her, Gino. Knock her block off. (*Etc.*)

ROBERTO. Get him, Connie. Show him who's boss. (*ETC.*)

(*At the peak of confusion CORRITA stands up and removes a pistol from her black purse. SHE fires two SHOTS into the air.*)

CORRITA. (*Wailing.*) STOP IT! I canna believe I raised such horrible children. (*Emotional.*) Somebody ina this room killed my husband. One-a my own flesh and blood killed my husband, God forbid.

GINO. Listen to the bleeding widow over here. None of us are impressed with your performance. You wanted the old man six feet under same as the rest of us.

CORRITA. (*Flicks a gesture at Gino like a curse and puts her gun away.*) God is gonna get you for that.

ROBERTO. (*Excited—jumping up and down.*) I got it! I got it! I got it! I got it! I got it! I got it!

CONNIE. Yeah, well, don't give it to me.

ROBERTO. We gotta think like Nancy Drew would think. Who had a motive to kill Papa?

(*Suddenly EVERYONE, but ROBERTO, bursts out laughing, long and hard.*)

CONNIE. (*Getting her breath back.*) That was a good one, kid.

CORRITA. We needed a little humor about right now.

GINO. Nice try, Roberto, but everyone in this room had a motive for rubbing out the old bastard.

(Suddenly the study door opens. VALARIA pushes her way into the room. SHE looks haggard. CONNIE crosses to desk as VALARIA comes down the stairs.)

CONNIE. Where've you been, Malaria?

VALARIA. *(Correcting.)* Valaria. *(Crossing to Gino.)* You're not gonna believe what happened to me, Gino.

GINO. Did you get the booze?

VALARIA. *(Wanders around in a state of shock. Upset.)* The liquor store got robbed while I was there. I was standing in line holding tree bottles of vodka, a case a scotch and some Galliano when this guy in a ski mask came in and robbed us. He took the money from the cash drawer. *(Begins to cry in squeaks.)* ... and then ... he robbed me. He took my purse. My purse. *(VALARIA sits on the sofa next to the dead Don.)*

GINO. So you didn't you get the booze?

VALARIA. *(Wailing.)* Do you know what I had in my purse? I can't believe it. He took it. *(VALARIA turns and sees the Don, but it doesn't register.)* I can't believe it. Just took it ... *(VALARIA buries her face in her hands, then suddenly turns to the dead Don and screams. SHE jumps and leaps away from the dead body.)* AGGGGGGGGGGGGGGHHHHHHHHHHHHHHHHHH. Is he?

CONNIE. Dead.

VALARIA. What happened?

BABY. Somebody murdered him.

CORRITA. Wait a minute. Something ain't right. I left the Don in his study. I walked down the hall going back to the party. I stopped for a second to look out the window at Sophia taking a picture of the grass. Then Baby passed me on her way back to the study.

BABY. I remember.

CORRITA. I left Papa alone. How could anyone have shot him? No one passed me in the hall 'cept Baby.

BABY. So, there was very little time from when you left him to when I found him.

CONNIE. (*Sarcastic.*) Maybe he realized the error of his ways and shot himself.

ROBERTO. Well that's stupid. He couldn't have shot himself in the back.

GINO. (*To Corrita.*) Maybe you rubbed him out, Mama.

CORRITA. What?

GINO. Why not? You hated him as much as we did.

CONNIE. Yeah and she was the last one to see him alive.

BABY. Shouldn't we be looking for Papa's will? I'd be real curious to know how much he left us.

CONNIE. (*Indicating the desk.*) It should be here somewhere.

GINO. Find it. (*To Corrita.*) What made you think you could get away with killing our father?

CORRITA. I canna believe I raised such greedy, selfish children.

(*CONNIE starts looking through desk. ONE-EYED JOE starts creeping up the stairs.*)

CONNIE. Mama, you made us in your own image. We're as rotten as you.

(CORRITA thinks about that for a beat or two and nods, agreeing with Connie.)

GINO. Connie, find that will.
CONNIE. I'm looking. I'm looking.

(ONE-EYED JOE opens the study door to escape.)

GINO. Hey, One-Eyed Joe. Get your ass down here. Youse a member of this family now. You know, as in richness, in poorness and in deathness.

ONE-EYED JOE. *(To Gino.)* With all the excitement I'm exhausted. I was hoping I coulda lay down for justa a half hour or so. *(Sobbing.)* I no feel too good. *(Points to Connie.)* She gonna hurt me.

GINO. You gotta show her who's boss. Keep her on her toes. Like this. Valaria!

VALARIA. What?

GINO. *(Hits Valaria in the back of the head. Sniffing around Joe.)* Knock her around some. Don't let her step on you. You smell good. What is that?

ONE-EYED JOE. *(Sobbing.)* It's called *Surrender*.

CORRITA. Enough! Roberto help One-Eyed Joe take Papa's body to the walk-in freezer in the basement until Uncle Vito comes.

ONE-EYED JOE. *(Squeal—looking at the dead Don.)* You wanna me to touch the deada Don?

ROBERTO. *(To Gino.)* And you call me a pansy.

(ONE-EYED JOE and ROBERTO grab hold of THE DON and exit. VALARIA goes to the phone and dials.)

GINO. I read a newspaper story once where this woman killed her husband for his money. She drugged him, stabbed him, diced him and buried him in her tomato garden. (*To Corrita.*) You make a pretty good spaghetti sauce, Ma. What's your secret?

CORRITA. AH! Shut up!

VALARIA. (*Into the phone.*) Hello? Police? My name is Valaria Cons ...

(*CORRITA is startled. CONNIE jumps back. GINO runs to her and pulls the phone out of her hand.*)

CORRITA. Policia!

CONNIE. (*To Gino as SHE resumes looking through the desk.*) You know how to pick 'em.

GINO. (*Interrupting.*) Stupid woman! What are you, crazy?

VALARIA. Me? I just got robbed and your father's been murdered, who the hell should I be calling? Domino's pizza?

GINO. We don't call no police in this family.

VALARIA. And what about his body? A funeral home's gonna want a death certificate.

(*CORRITA wails and throws herself on the dead Don. BABY console her. CORRITA cradles the Don's head in her arms.*)

GINO. We own funeral homes. Get it?

VALARIA. Got it.

GINO. Good. Sit in the corner and try to look pretty.

(ROBERTO enters and crosses to Corrita.)

CONNIE. Wishful thinking.

VALARIA. What about my robbery? That gunman took something very valuable to me. What am I gonna do?

GINO. Money? Jewelry? What?

VALARIA. It was ... (*Realizes she can't say what it really was.*) It was from my aunt. Yeah, Aunt Rita. It was ... uh ... bracelets. Yeah, bracelets.

GINO. Bracelets??

VALARIA. Two gold bracelets with diamonds and rubies.

CONNIE. (*Opening a drawer.*) Ahh! HA!

GINO. You found the will?

CONNIE. No, but Papa's gun is missing.

(CONNIE looks over to ROBERTO who gets frightened.)

CONNIE. I wonder what happened to it. (*Walks to Roberto.*) I wonder if it was the murder weapon. (*Pause.*) I wonder who knew it was there in the first place.

ROBERTO. (*Nervous.*) Well ... uh ... I agree with Gino. I think Mama killed Papa.

CORRITA. (*Dropping the Don's head.*) That's it! I've had enough of these fingers in my faze. I'm taking charge of this family right now. And I'm gonna remain in charge until a will is found telling me otherwise.

GINO. (*To Corrita.*) Soooooooooooooo. We hit a nerve?

CORRITA. Shut up. Shut up all of youse. Now you gonna listen to what I gotta say. Get this true your fat heads I am innocent for this simple reason. (*Crosses to*

CENTER STAGE.) If I could survive forty years of blood splattered laundry and not kill your Papa before today I shouldn't even come under suspect. Besides. For forty years I've been killing him slowly with tons of pasta, butter, cheese, white bread and oil. So, I could have easily waited a few more years until his cholesterol level exploded. And then, no jury in the world could convict me.

ALL. (*Improvise.*) Yeah. Makes sense. Geez forty years. Wow. Yeah. I agree. Mama's innocent.

CORRITA. (*Slaps Roberto in the head.*) That's better. Now I suggest we put our heads on and try to figure out who killed the Don. The windows don't open. I was in the hall way and no one but Baby passed me. There is no other way into this room. How could someone have killed Papa?

GINO. What about a secret passageway?

(ROBERTO, CONNIE, BABY and VALARIA abruptly turn to Gino.)

CONNIE. Stupid idea.
ROBERTO. Bad idea.
CONNIE. Stupid idea.
BABY. Whata you think this is? The movies?
VALARIA. (*Laughing.*) A secret passageway. How funny.
CONNIE. Stupid idea.
GINO. Does anyone know there isn't a secret passageway in this room?

(ROBERTO, CONNIE, BABY and VALARIA abruptly turn away from Gino.)

CORRITA. Connie! What's matter for you? You look like you swallowed the cat that ate the canoli. Do you know of such a thing as a secret passage way ina this room?

CONNIE. No, Mama. I ain't ever see one.

CORRITA. Baby?

BABY. What?

CORRITA. What do you mean? What? Answer the question.

BABY. (*Bad liar.*) No. I ain't seen anything like that.

ROBERTO. (*Guilty.*) Me neither.

GINO. Mama, when Baby passed you in the hall couldn't she have gone in and just shot Papa and said she found the body?

BABY. (*Shocked.*) GINO? How could you suggest that I'd...?

GINO. You're such an actress. I'm surprised you haven't stampeded us getting to the phone to find out if that role Papa made you give up is still available.

BABY. For your information that role went to a fellow Italian, Beth-Ann Maxwelloni. But there will be other, greater roles for moi to breathe life into. The Don is dead. Long live ... (*Shaking her body.*) BA-BY GIO-VANI!!! (*Serious.*) But I didn't kill the son-of-a-bitch, Mama.

CONNIE. If there was a secret passageway to this room, and I ain't saying there is, Roberto could have shot Papa after Mama left, using the secret passageway. (*To Roberto.*) I keep wondering where Papa's gun could have gotten to.

ROBERTO. If there is, in fact, a secret passageway, and I am not saying there is a secret passageway, but I am not saying there isn't a secret passageway, ANYONE, including you, Connie, could have used the secret passageway ...

CORRITA. (*Interrupting—holding her hands to her head.*) Stop already with the secret passageway crap. I feel like a character from *Clue.*

VALARIA. (*Prissy impersonation.*) Miss Scarlett. Miss Scarlett! I don't know nothing 'bout no secret passageway.

CONNIE. Hilarious Malaria.

VALARIA. (*Sarcastic.*) That joke is wearing thin, Constance!

CONNIE. You don't wanna mess with me.

GINO. All right. All right. Break it up. We agree Mama's innocent. We agree, huh?

(*Ad libs "Yeah. Okay. Sure. Yeah. Get off my back."*)

VALARIA. And me. I was at the liquor store getting robbed.

GINO. Do we all agree, then? Mama and Valaria are innocent.

CONNIE. I wanna check out the bimbo's story.

GINO.Why? She ain't got no motive.

(*In regards to the above, BABY suddenly gets this pained expression on her face.*)

BABY. I gotta go think. (*BABY runs up the stairs and out the study door.*)

CONNIE. That's a first.

CORRITA. Gino, Connie, go upstairs and tell all the guests to geta the hell outta here. Maybe your Uncle Vito knows where the will is.

(GINO and VALARIA walk out.)

CONNIE. (To Corrita.) Uh ... You gonna be okay, Mama.
CORRITA. Nobody's ever died from a broken heart.

(CONNIE, a little worried, eyes the secret panel on her way out.)

CORRITA. I justa need to be alone for a time. Close the door will you. (As soon as the door closes CORRITA crosses to the desk and grabs the the phone. SHE dials. Running her hand over the volumes of books in the book shelf, SHE listens to the rings and sings song from a 'fairy tale.) I got'a no stings to keepa me down. To keepa me-a on the ground. (Into the phone.) Hello? Disney World? I wanta one way ticket to the Magic Kingdom. Hold? Sure. I've been on hold for forty years. Another few minutes ain't gonna kill me. (Sings.) Ding dong the don is dead. Da la la. La la. (SHE continues running her finger over the books and turns to look at them. In same row as the trigger book that opens the panel CORRITA reads titles.) Italian Music to Make Love By. (Looking up.) He never used that with me. (Reading.) The Sensuous Man. (CORRITA bursts out laughing.) Oh. That's a good one. (Reading.) The Path to My Mistress. (Grabbing book.) Now wait justa damn a minute ... (SHE pulls the trigger book and the secret panel pops open. CORRITA steps back in *amazement.)* I'll be a son-of-bitch. *(SHE puts the phone to her mouth—excited.)* Mickey! I'll call you back. *(SHE hangs up the phone.)* I donna believe this. *(CORRITA steps into the passageway and closes it.)*

(The study door opens and BABY enters. SHE runs to the phone and dials. Her voice remains cheery and bright and understanding, but her facial features betray her hate for this girl.)

BABY. *(Like a Valley girl.)* Hello? Beth-Ann, like, how are you. This is Baby Giovani. I'm fine, and you? Good. Not much, well, except for the fact that my father died this afternoon. Bummer, I know. I'll make this short and sweet. How much money do you want for dropping out of my role. *(BABY'S face drops to the floor.)* No problem. Okay, like, we'll do lunch tomorrow and I'll give it to you then. You too. Bye. *(Screaming.)* Bitch!!! *(Frantically BABY begins searching through the desk for the will.)* Where is it? It's got to be here. I need money. AGHHHHHH!!!! *(Gives up.)* Son-of-a-bitch!

ROBERTO. *(Enters the study.)* There you are. I've looked everywhere for you.

BABY. What do you want!

ROBERTO. I need a favor.

BABY. What?

ROBERTO. Tell everyone I was with you until you discovered Papa's body.

BABY. Roberto, I ain't a liar.

ROBERTO. Don't think of it as lying. Think of it as an acting exercise. All you gotta say is that I was with you when you were looking for the photographer.

BABY. But you weren't with me.

ROBERTO. But I could have been.

BABY. Not if you were murdering Papa.

ROBERTO. Oh, Baby, you can't think that. I pass out when I get a nose bleed.

BABY. Where were you then?

ROBERTO. I can't tell.

BABY. Why not?

ROBERTO. Baby, please, you just gotta believe me. You gotta help me. Trust me.

BABY. Trust you? If I say you was with me the whole time, what am I gonna say to Gino who was really with me. He'll know you weren't with me.

ROBERTO. We'll tell everyone that we were with each other and that Gino is lying. Mama'll never trusts Gino. She hates him.

BABY. I'd be hurting Gino.

ROBERTO. Like he hurt you before? Accusing you of Papa's murder?

BABY. That is true.

ROBERTO. Besides, Gino's a big man. He can take care of himself.

BABY. (*Thinks.*) All right. I'll help you.

ROBERTO. Oh, thanks, Baby. You're a life saver.

BABY. I'll lie for you, but I'm not doing it out of love or respect for you. I'm not doing it for the old family honor system. I'm doing it because of trust. I trust you ... will give me three thousand dollars and not a cent less.

ROBERTO. What?

BABY. You don't like my terms? (*Yelling.*) Hey! MAAAAAAAAAAAAAMMMMMMMMMMAAAAAA AAAAAA!

ROBERTO. Okay. Okay. Shut up! I'll give you the money. Jeez! You can't trust anyone.

BLACKOUT

End of Scene 1

ACT II

Scene 2

AT RISE: A half an hour has passed. CONNIE enters the study and slowly crosses to the bar. SHE removes her veil and tosses it on the sofa and kicks off her shoes, one by one. CONNIE looks around the room with memory-filled eyes.

CONNIE. (*Lamenting.*) It's the end of an era, huh, Papa? (*Pours herself a drink.*) You were the last of a dying breed. Time marched right across your life. You became nothing but a D.P. in the stream of technology. A relic. A Louis the Fourteenth desk in a room full of bean-bag chairs. (*CONNIE turns around and talks to the desk.*) Is that why you were so mean and bitter toward the end? The world changed and you didn't. You must have really hated it all. I still remember the day when Rat Chow Charlie got an earring. (*Laughs.*) You tried to beat him up 'cause you thought he turned sissy. (*Smiles.*) For years you thought an Uzi was a Greek wine. (*CONNIE raises her glass.*)

Here's to you, Donald Giovani ... Papa. The last godfather. (*CONNIE downs her drink in one shot, places the glass on the bar and slowly walks to the desk.*) You were such an impressive character behind this desk. You were so big when I was small. So menacing and commanding one minute and then you'd look at me and melt. (*CONNIE goes around in back of the desk and touches the chair.*) I've always wanted to be like you. (*With a smile.*) I knew you were hauling in your girlfriends true that secret passageway since I was ten. Nothing got past me. That's why when Rocky and I starting seeing each other I had him come in the same way. Tradition!

(*ONE-EYED JOE enters quietly. HE watches and listens to Connie.*)

CONNIE. You would have liked Rocky. He was a lot like you. In many ways he was trying to preserve your world. Family honor, tradition and respect meant something to him. Well, in a warped sort of nowadays way. He even owned a fedora. And then you killed him. And then somebody killed you. (*Pause.*) I'm gonna miss you, you son-of-a-bitch.

ONE-EYED JOE. I wonder ...

CONNIE. (*Whips around. Nasty.*) What the hell are you doing here, mutant face? Spying on me? Listening where you ain't suppose to?

ONE-EYED JOE. I'm a sorry if I upset you ...

CONNIE. And you're a pretty sorry sight.

ONE-EYED JOE. Everyone isa coming back here. I listen to what you say about your papa and I like. Many people will miss him I'm sure. I'm sorry he got killed.

CONNIE. Thanks. I've been a real bitch *hag* to you. Haven't I?

ONE-EYED JOE. No. No.

CONNIE. We dragged you to a shotgun wedding, but it's over now. I'm not really gonna sue you. I just said that.

ONE-EYED JOE. Thank you. Connie, I was a wondering. When you said just now you gonna miss the son-of-a-bitch. Which son-of-a-bitch did you mean?

CONNIE. Go pour me a drink.

(ONE-EYED JOE crosses to bar.)

CONNIE. Both of 'em. They were a lot alike in many ways. The first fifteen years I spent with Papa, the last with Rocky. I must've spent a total of three years by myself. I'm sorry they're gone, but I'm ... also kind of glad, too. Do you think that's bad?

ONE-EYED JOE. No. I donna think it's bad.

CONNIE. Now there are no bosses. No masters. Just Connie.

ONE-EYED JOE. *(Handing her a drink.)* They'll be another man. There always is.

(CONNIE takes drinks and stares off to space thinking. She is not sure whether she wants another man. JOE/ROCKY stares at her wondering, disturbed at what she might be thinking.)

CONNIE. *(Changing subject too quickly.)* I have to take care of business now. Gino is too stupid to run an empire. And the first order of business is to find out who killed Papa.

ONE-EYED JOE. It could have been one of the Malone gang?

CONNIE. No. Rocky's gang has class. They don't shoot people in the back. They kill people honorably.

ONE-EYED JOE. So you believe it was one of us in the house who killed the Don.

CONNIE. I think maybe Roberto. I saw him with a gun once and I think he hated Papa more than all of us combined. (*Toast.*) Good-bye, old man.

ONE-EYED JOE. Donna be sad, Connie. When you live by the sword you die by it. We all know that when we become members.

CONNIE. You know, you're not such a smuck after all.

ONE-EYED JOE. (*Laughs.*) I'm so glad we're not getting married. (*Pause.*) I had no idea what I was gonna say to my Antonio if we had.

CONNIE. Who's Antonio?

(*ONE-EYED JOE smiles rather impishly. CONNIE is at first confused, then realizes Antonio is his "boyfriend." SHE bursts out laughing.*)

CONNIE. Boy, Papa wasn't taking any chances.

(*GINO enters followed by ROBERTO, BABY and VALARIA. BABY is spraying whipped cream in her mouth.*)

ROBERTO. The guests are all gone.

BABY. Except Aunt Sophia. She's taking pictures of the caterer. (*BABY sprays some more whipped cream into her mouth.*)

GINO. I spoke with Uncle Vito about Papa's will.

CONNIE. What did he say?

GINO. He thinks it's hidden in a book.

CONNIE. (*Looking at bookcases.*) Oh, God. We'll be here all day.

(*BABY sits next to Connie on the sofa. VALARIA sits on the end of the desk. GINO starts looking through the bookshelf STAGE RIGHT. ROBERTO moves the chair back behind the desk. BABY begins sniffing the air. Something smells bad.*)

VALARIA. I love reading. It broadens one's mind.

ROBERTO. James Joyce. H. G. Wells. Agatha Christie.

VALARIA. Harold Robbins, Jackie Susann and Joan Collins.

(*BABY sniffs the air closer to Connie. BABY moves away from Connie.*)

ROBERTO. (*Gravely. To Valaria.*) If people were inanimate objects you'd be a used stamp.

VALARIA. No. I see myself more as a princess phone.

CONNIE. (*Groaning directed to Valaria.*) Ahhhhh!! What are we waiting for?

GINO. Mama.

VALARIA. Speaking of books, don't you guys feel like we're in a plot? I think it's all terribly exciting and thrilling. A wedding, a robbery, a missing will and a dead corpse.

CONNIE. (*Loses complete control, leaps off the sofa and darts for Valaria's throat.*) Let me at her!!!!!

(GINO and BABY grab on to CONNIE and prevent her from doing any real damage. GINO picks CONNIE up and moves her to opposite side of stage.)

CONNIE. I have had enough of her! Get her outta my face. Get her outta my house. Get her outta my life.

GINO. Connie, calm down. Mama should be here any minute.

CONNIE. I'm getting sick and tired of you always picking me up, like I was a lawn ornament or something.

GINO. (*Puts her down.*) You gotta watch your temper, sis.

(CONNIE slaps Gino across the face.)

GINO. That didn't hurt 'cause I know how upset you are.

CONNIE. (*Slaps Gino again.*) Did it hurt?

GINO. It hurt.

CONNIE. Good! 'Cause you're stupid, Gino. (*Marches to bookcases.*) Now tell me the name of the ~~goddamn~~ *For Heaven's* book we're suppose to look for?

GINO. The women in this family ... ~~Jesus~~ ... (*Pause.*) The will is hidden in a book called *Something to My Mistress.*

(VALARIA suddenly looks guilty. CONNIE's eyes light up guilty. SHE and ROBERTO exchange glances. THEY know that book well. CONNIE tries to act inconspicuous, but fails.)

CONNIE. Really? Well, I think I'll look over here. *(CONNIE goes right for the STAGE LEFT bookcase knowing where it is.)*
GINO. Valaria and Robert, help Connie. *(Pointing to STAGE RIGHT book cases.)* One-Eyed Joe and Baby, look with me.

(JOE and GINO look in earnest while BABY keeps peeking over at VALARIA, ROBERTO and CONNIE who are just standing around. VALARIA and CONNIE have a stare down contest—ROBERTO stands in the middle when it nearly gets out of hand. After a while BABY stops looking and just stares at Connie and company. GINO catches her.)

GINO. Baby, what are you ...

(GINO turns around and sees VALARIA, ROBERTO and CONNIE just staring at nothing.)

GINO. What the hell is going ...
CONNIE. *(Interrupting/mock surprise.)* Gino! Gosh. Look! *The Path to My Mistress*. Could this be it?
GINO. *(Crossing to Connie.)* Get outta my way. I'll handle this.

*(EVERYONE clears out of his way. GINO tries to pull the
    book out but fails.)*

GINO. It won't come out.
CONNIE. Gee, Gino. Why don't you try to pull it in a
downward motion. It's probably stuck.

*(With the greatest of ease GINO pulls down on the book.
    The secret panel pops open. BABY, ROBERTO
    CONNIE and VALARIA overplay their surprise at
    discovering the passageway.)*

BABY, ROBERTO, VALARIA and CONNIE. Wow.
Gee. Imagine that. I can't believe it. Awesome.
GINO. Maybe I'm smarter than I think.

*(As the panel swings open CORRITA is revealed. SHE is
    standing with a smug expression on her face and carries
    a black glove.)*

CORRITA. So youse all not as stupid as I thought you
were.
CONNIE. Not us, Mama. Gino found it.
ROBERTO. Yeah.
BABY. All by himself.
VALARIA. Like he knew where it was.
GINO. Mama, what are you doing in there?
CORRITA. I'm looking for clues.
ROBERTO. (*Guilty.*) Did you find any?
CORRITA. Your Papa used this secret passageway to
smuggle his girlfriends into this house. That son-of-a-
bitch!

BABY. How do you know that?

CORRITA. The tunnels are cluttered with used cosmetics, empty hair spray cans, fake eyelashes and lots of ripped panty hose. It's like-a a prostitute exploded in there.

BABY. (*Thinking aloud.*) So Papa's mistresses used that tunnel? (*BABY looks at Valaria.*)

CORRITA. But the killer used it too. (*Holding up gloves.*) This is evidence. I believe the killer wore it when he shot the Don. I found gunpowder burns on it. I also found make-up stains. Fortunately I recognized the make-up, Party Girl skin tone number four. It's called Virgin Bride.

(*CONNIE, VALARIA and BABY suddenly get nervous.*)

GINO. That means Roberto and I are innocent!

ROBERTO. Yeah! That ain't my color.

(*GINO throws Roberto a dirty look.*)

ROBERTO. I use it to hide my zits. Okay!

(*GINO steps away from Roberto slowly.*)

CORRITA. (*Walks up to Connie.*) I've seen this shade of make-up before. (*Walks up to Baby.*) I've seen it recently too. (*Turns to Valaria.*) You got it caked onto you face like a cheap whore from the boulevard.

VALARIA. Hey! I don't work the boulevard no more.

GINO. Mama. It ain't Valaria. She's got an alibi.

VALARIA. Yeah! I got robbed.

CONNIE. (*Wicked.*) Oh, my God. I forgot all about it. Mama. I called the liquor store where Little Miss Innocent over there allegedly got robbed. They haven't had a robbery in days.

CORRITA and GINO. What?

VALARIA. That's a lie! She's just saying that 'cause she doesn't like me.

(*BABY begins jumping up and down excited with the information she has to contribute.*)

GINO. Connie?

CONNIE. It's true I don't like her. BUT why would I lie about something you can check out in two seconds?

GINO. (*To Valaria.*) Where were you!

CORRITA. But, Gino, what's her motive?

VALARIA. I ain't got any.

BABY. (*Bursting.*) Her and Papa were entwined in the unholy bond of adulthood.

ALL. (*Shock and perhaps amusement.*) What? Huh? You gotta be kidding. (*Etc.*)

BABY. (*Bursting—quickly.*) I saw her and Papa talking in this very room about an hour before the Don's demise. I was spying, see. She knows about the secret passageway 'cause that's how Papa let her out. She was his mistress!

CONNIE. So, little Miss "Oldest Profession" over here ain't got an alibi, her make-up was found on the glove and she knew about the secret passageway. I'm convinced. Hang her.

GINO. You and my father?

CORRITA. (*To Valaria.*) Is what Baby says true?

VALARIA. Your husband, Mrs. Don, wanted to make it clear to me that I wasn't never to see Gino again. He opened the secret passageway because it led out to the mausoleum close to the liquor store. That's all!

CONNIE. HA!

CORRITA. *(To Valaria.)* That's all?

VALARIA. That's all. And as for the rest of my alibi, Gino. Why don't you be a man and call the damn liquor store. Connie's lying! Can't you see that?

CONNIE. I am not lying.

(GINO crosses to the phone. CONNIE starts smiling. GINO picks up the phone and dials. CONNIE breaks out laughing.)

GINO. *(Intensely staring at Connie.)* You are lying.

(CONNIE continues laughing.)

VALARIA. I told you.

CORRITA. *(Hits Connie in the back of the head.)* What the hell's a matter for you? You crazy?

CONNIE. Ah! I just wanted to see the bimbo sweat a little, so what!

VALARIA. *(Very high-brow.)* If you'll excuse me. I'm going to freshen up. *(With dignity VALARIA walks up the stairs. Turning back.)* Where's the john again?

CORRITA. Down the hall and to your right.

(VALARIA exits.)

CORRITA. *(To Gino.)* Can't you do any better?

GINO. (*Ignoring Corrita.*) All right. So, Ma, Valaria and I are innocent.

ROBERTO. Why is Gino innocent?

GINO. 'Cause I don't wear make-up.

CORRITA. I'm not ruling you out, Gino Giovani.

GINO. You wouldn't.

CONNIE. So, we're back to square one and we still ain't got the will.

GINO. I can't understand it. Uncle Vito was sure it was in the book *A Path to My Mistress.*

CORRITA. (*Indicating book.*) It's a dummy. (*To Gino.*) Like-a you.

BABY. Well, maybe the will is somewhere in the passageway. Shouldn't we look?

CORRITA. It ain't in there, Baby. I searched every inch.

CONNIE. Wait a minute. Wait a minute. Baby. Baby.

BABY. (*Becomes terrified.*) What?

CONNIE. If you saw Valaria go through the secret panel that means you must have known about it.

CORRITA. Again witha the secret passageways?

GINO. That's right.

BABY This is why I didn't tell you about Valaria before because I knew you would accuse me.

CONNIE. Baby murdered Papa. It all makes sense.

BABY. I saw that secret panel for the first time today.

GINO. An hour before, as you so aptly put it, the Don's demise. (*Reconstructing the crime.*) Seeing the passageway, you saw light at the end of your own suppressed life. In a moment of passion you seized the opportunity to kill Papa thus freeing yourself to pursue a tawdry life in the theater.

BABY. And they call me dramatic.

CORRITA. That's a no good. Diz tunnel splits three ways. One way to the basement, one way upstairs and the other goes to the mausoleum in the backyard. I left Papa and five minutes later I saw Baby in the hallway. She couldn't have shot Papa, climbed the tunnel ladder to the upstairs, ran downstairs in time to meet me ina the hall. She would have been out of breath and sweating like-a pig.

BABY. I never thought I'd live to see the day I'd be happy I was overweight. (*SHE squirts whipped cream in her mouth.*)

ONE-EYED JOE. I am many things, Mrs. Giovani, but in shape is not one of them. I couldn't do that much running.

GINO. So, Valaria, Mama, Baby and me are innocent.

CORRITA. Quit including yourself in the innocent category, Gino.

ONE-EYED JOE. What about me?

CORRITA. I haven't decided about you. (*Turns to Connie.*) Or you.

CONNIE. (*Calm and cool.*) When I left this room after the picture-taking fiasco, Joe and I headed up to mingle. I talked to Nick the Fish's wife, Melia, and Mrs. Harris. The reluctant groom was three steps behind me at all times smelling like a day old clambake on Cape Cod. Ain't that right, Joe?

ONE-EYED JOE. It is.

GINO. (*To Connie.*) You two have gotten awfully chummy.

ROBERTO. (*To Corrita.*) Mama, did you find anything else in the tunnels?

CORRITA. You mean like a hundred or so crumpled up pieces of paper with half written poems on them?

ROBERTO. Uh ... er ... Gee ... I wasn't ... necessary thinking of anything specifically specific?

CORRITA. Either Lord Byron's alive and well and writing the worst poetry of his career or ...

GINO. (*Interrupting. Charging to Roberto.*) Roberto knew about the tunnel all along too! How come I'm the only one in this family who didn't know?

CORRITA. You was never too bright, Gino.

GINO. That means Roberto could be Papa's killer too.

CORRITA. He's not a killer. Sissies don't kill.

CONNIE. (*Her ears perk up on that word.*) Yeah, but sissies shoot people in the back.

ROBERTO. I wasn't the only one who knew about the tunnels. (*Pointing to Connie.*) She knew about 'em too.

CONNIE. (*Raising her hand.*) I ought to ...

CORRITA. (*Catches Connie's hand.*) Donna you strike that child.

CONNIE. What child! He's twenty-three years old.

BABY. The plot thickens.

CONNIE. So what. Everyone knew about the tunnels except Mama and Gino. Let's talk murder weapon. Ask Roberto where Papa's gun is. I caught him aiming it out of the secret panel once like he was practicing to shoot someone.

CORRITA. (*To Roberto.*) Is this true?

ROBERTO. Yes, but ...

CORRITA. Gino, go up and search Roberto's room.

CONNIE. I'm convinced. Hang him!

ROBERTO. (*Stands in Gino's way. Yelling.*) No.

CORRITA. Why not.

ROBERTO. I ... uh ... just ... cleaned it?
CORRITA. (*To Gino.*) Go.

(GINO heads for the stairs and ROBERTO leaps on Gino's legs. GINO steps up the stairs dragging ROBERTO behind as HE speaks.)

ROBERTO. There ain't ... anything of ... interest to anyone ... up there ...
CONNIE. It all makes perfect sense to me. He wanted that money for poetry school so bad he went ahead and bumped off the old man for it.
ROBERTO. I HAVE AN ALIBI.

(GINO stops. VALARIA enters.)

CORRITA. If you got something to say, son, say it.
ROBERTO. Tell 'em, Baby.
BABY. (*Smiles and takes CENTER STAGE. Rehearsed—like an actress.*) Well, after Mama sent me up to look for the photographer I found Roberto and we stayed together until he headed to the tortellini table and I went back to the study.
CORRITA. So, Roberto wouldn't have had enough time.
CONNIE. We're running out of suspects.
GINO. Hey, wait a minute. (*Realizing.*) That's my alibi. I was with you, Baby.
ROBERTO. I didn't see you.
GINO. Of course you didn't. You weren't with us. Was he, Baby?
BABY. I was with Roberto.

ROBERTO. That's right.

GINO. That's bullshit.

CONNIE (*To Gino.*) I'm convinced. Hang GINO, but for God sake hang somebody.

GINO. I was with Baby.

BABY. (*Smiling.*) Were not.

GINO. Was too.

ROBERTO. Were not.

CONNIE. (*Disbelief.*) You bumped off Papa over 976?

GINO. I didn't know about the secret panel until today.

ROBERTO. We said we didn't know about it either. You could be lying too.

BABY. If you can murder your own father, lying is not beneath you.

GINO. I didn't kill him.

CORRITA. Go to your room, Gino. Roberto and Baby see that he stays there until I make some calls.

(GINO, BABY and ROBERTO exit.)

CORRITA. Hey, Joe take-a Malaria up to the kitchen and feed her something will ya?

(JOE and VALARIA exit)

CORRITA. The make-up, the secret panel, the glove, the robbery at the liquor store. Who killed the Don?

CONNIE. Gino. Let's hang him.

CORRITA. It's not like Gino to be caught without an alibi. Papa raised him better than that.

CONNIE. If Gino didn't do it, who's left?

CORRITA. I'm not so sure it's a who dunnit as much as it's a how they dunnit.

CONNIE. I don't understand.

CORRITA. There's a piece of the puzzle missing from all of this, Connie, and I intend to finda out what it is.

CONNIE. Maybe it's the will?

CORRITA. No. (*Removes the will from her dress pocket.*) I found that in the tunnel.

CONNIE. (*Excited.*) You've got the will. Who did he leave it to, Mama? Oh, God, tell me.

CORRITA. The house and money to me. The business to Gino.

CONNIE. (*Screaming.*) GINO!!!!!

CORRITA. You gotta have faith, Connie.

CONNIE. (*In agony.*) Faith? How can you talk about faith? Gino doesn't even want the business.

CORRITA. Connie. I demand that you have faith in your old mother.

CONNIE. Okay. I have faith in you, Mama. Now what?

(*CORRITA rips the will in a thousand pieces.*)

BLACKOUT

End of Scene 2

ACT II

Scene 3

AT RISE: Two hours have passed. CONNIE is chain-smoking sitting at the desk. ONE-EYED JOE is sitting in a reception chair eating.

CONNIE. Mama said she had some investigating to do and a call to make. I hope this is over quickly I wanna get out of this dress and into a hot tub.

ONE-EYED JOE. They have Gino chained up.

CONNIE. You're kidding?

ONE-EYED JOE. Roberto was afraid Gino might become violent so they handcuffed him.

CONNIE. That was stupid. Gino's been getting out of handcuffs since high school.

ONE-EYED JOE. That's what Roberto said and, well ... Gino ain't gonna get outta this.

CONNIE. What do you mean?

(GINO enters/hops in. His left wrist is handcuffed to his left ankle. VALARIA is helping him to balance. HE slowly takes the stairs by hopping down each one individually. HE is humiliated beyond belief.)

GINO. (*Deep growling.*) When I get outta of these, Roberto I'm gonna ...

ROBERTO. If you start hurtling insults at me, Gino, I'll tape your mouth again. (*ROBERTO removes a roll of masking tape.*)

CONNIE. I gotta see that. Insult him, Gino. Please.

GINO. (*Growling.*) Grrrrrrrrrrrrrrrrrrrr.

(*VALARIA and GINO hop/walk to sofa.*)

CONNIE. (*Teasing.*) No fast moves now, Gino.

(*BABY appears at the door with a gun in her hand acting like a police woman.*)

GINO. And here comes Baby Eastwood.

BABY. Mama, told me to keep an eye open for anything strange.

CONNIE. Stay away from mirrors.

GINO. She's got my old BB gun, for God's sake. What are you going to do, BB someone to death?

CONNIE. Where's Mama?

BABY. She's on the phone to Nick the Fish's wife.

ROBERTO. If Gino killed Papa how will the family punish him?

CONNIE. (*Indicating Valaria.*) I would imagine going out with someone like her is punishment enough.

VALARIA. Don't push me, Giovani. I ain't in the mood.

CONNIE. No one's ever in the mood for getting their face bashed in.

VALARIA. You know for two cents I'd wallpaper this room with you.

ROBERTO. (*Thinking.*) Wallpaper. Now that's an idea. I've often felt a touch of mauve in this room would be wonderful.

(*CONNIE pushes Roberto out of her way.*)

CONNIE. For fifty cents I could do liposuction on your face. It might help.

GINO. I got a buck in my pocket, why don't you kill each other.

CONNIE. It scares you to think the old man might have left the empire to me, doesn't it?

GINO. Even if he did, Papa's boys ain't gonna listen to you.

(CONNIE struts across the stage to the sofa. SHE places her leg on the sofa to adjust her wedding garter.)

CONNIE. (*Sexy.*) I guess you've forgotten that men have a way of listening when a lady talks.

GINO. Why the hell do you wanna rule the family business, anyway? You're a woman. Don't you want a family. Kids?

ONE-EYED JOE. What about a husband to take care of you?

CONNIE. I don't need a man to take care of me. I want this business to take care of me. That's all that's ever mattered to me. It's in my blood. Baby don't care and neither does Roberto, God forbid. Gino sees it as capital for his business ventures, but me, I see it as a way of life. Papa lived and died for it. (*CONNIE takes this very seriously.*) You're just a second rate hood, Joe. (*CONNIE takes CENTER STAGE.*) You couldn't possible understand how I feel.

(CORRITA enters. SHE carries a large bag and a suit case. SHE puts them down and listens.)

CONNIE. Love, children, a man ... a family? You wouldn't ask me if I wanted those things if you knew that this business is my family. And I'm not talking about who's related to who. I'm talking about a group of people who rely on each other's experience and knowledge. A network of people who come together to overcome the odds. It's such a good gut feeling ... it could only be criminal. And among these criminals and thieves there is honor. The honor of this family is something I can feel, trust and believe in. The Giovani family has always been a part of the tradition of crime since the dawn of creation. Our family tree includes Lucrezia Borgia and prominent members of the Spanish Inquisition. One of the men who stabbed Caesar was a Giovani. I am proud to be sixth generation in the family business and I am very proud to be the daughter of a Don. *(Beat.)* Besides what sounds better? Connie Malone —Rocky's wife or ... *(Big and dramatic.)* Connie Giovani—Mafia Queen.

CORRITA. *(Has burst out crying. SHE runs to Connie.)* Your Papa would have been so proud, Connie. You two always fought like cats and dogs because you were cut from the same cloth. I'm so proud.

(ONE-EYED JOE views her much differently. HE steps away there is a disappointment in his demeanor.)

BABY. Gosh, Connie when they do your life story I gotta play you.

CONNIE. Lose some weight, first.

ROBERTO. I didn't know there was so much poetic inspiration in the mob.

(CORRITA grabs her suitcase and large bag and goes to the desk. If there is anyone there she kicks them out.)

CORRITA. Everybody listen to me. I know who the killer is and I gotta tell you if your Papa knew who killed him he'd die.

GINO. It ain't me. It ain't me.

CORRITA. You ain't got an alibi, Gino. Your Papa would be very disappointed.

GINO. I didn't do it.

ROBERTO. I got an alibi.

CORRITA. *(Hits Roberto in back of head.)* So you've said, Shakespeare, but when I was in the tunnels I found a panel which led to your room. It was right by those crumpled up pieces of poetry. In your room I found some interesting things.

ROBERTO. I was with Baby. I didn't kill, Papa.

(CORRITA reaches into her bag and removes a gun.)

CONNIE. It's Papa's gun, ain't it?

CORRITA. *(Turns to Roberto.)* Guess where I found it.

ROBERTO. *(Guilty.)* Rolled up in cloth stuffed in a shopping bag which was wrapped with Christmas paper and hid under boxes and boxes of personal poetry in the back of my walk-in closet?

BABY. My God, Mama. You're good.

CORRITA. I've been watching *Kojak* for years.

ROBERTO. Now, Mama I can explain.

CONNIE. I'm convinced. Hang him.

ROBERTO. Tell 'em, Baby.

CORRITA. Baby?

BABY. (*Hysterical.*) Do any of you know how difficult it is to be a fat actress?

ROBERTO. BABY!

BABY. We gotta work twice as hard as the beauty queens. I needed that three thousand dollars.

GINO. What the hell is she talking about?

CONNIE. She's sounds guilty.

ROBERTO. I don't know what she's talking about, Mama, but she's my alibi. She promised and I already gave her the money.

CORRITA. (*Goes digging in her bag again.*) Ifa what you say is true, Roberto, you are the only person I ever met who coulda be ina two places at the same time. (CORRITA removes a pink handbag, Valaria's.)

VALARIA. That's my handbag.

(*VALARIA goes for it. CORRITA slaps her hands away.*)

CORRITA. That's evidence.

VALARIA. How'd you find it?

CONNIE. Where'd you find it?

ROBERTO. Wrapped in birthday paper, stuffed in a brief case and tossed into an old suit case in the back of my walk-in closet.

CORRITA. Any minute I expected Jimmy Hoffa to pop up ina the back of that walk-in closet of his.

BABY. So Roberto's the murderer?

VALARIA. (*Goes for handbag.*) Corrita, can I have my handbag back?

CORRITA. (*Slaps Valaria's hands again.*) I'ma not gonna tell you again. No. (*To Baby.*) No, Baby. Roberto isa no murder. He's the robber. (*CORRITA takes CENTER STAGE*.) Roberto flew outta here like a shot, went to his room, got his gun and used the passage way to the mausoleum. He went to the liquor store and robbed it. Am I right?

(Dead silence.
EVERYONE turns to Roberto—HE freaks out.)

ROBERTO. (*Sobbing*.) Yes. Yes. I robbed the liquor store. I've been practicing holding a gun for weeks. I needed the money for poetry school. I'm so sorry.

(Suddenly EVERYONE bursts into applause and surrounds Roberto with congratulations.)

CORRITA. Your papa would have been so proud of you. His first arrest came from a liquor store hold-up.

CONNIE. Maybe there is a Giovani buried some where inside him.

GINO. Don't bet on it. One robbery don't mean a thing. (*Pause*.) So Baby, maybe you can tell the truth now.

BABY. Mama, I was with Gino and I feel awful about it.

CORRITA. I feel awful when I'ma with Gino too.

GINO. I told you I was innocent, Mama. Now, somebody get these cuffs off of me.

CORRITA. I always knew you were innocent, big shot. Aunt Sophia had taken a polaroid of you and Baby.

GINO. (*Anger building*.) Get me outta these cuffs.

CORRITA. No. Lately, you been really obnoxious, mister big shot. More than that you been rude to me for no reason. I raised you like you was my own. I never treated you any different than my own children. That was in your mind. Lately, you've gotten it into your head that I was some kind of evil step-mother. Bullshit! You're all upset because you don't know the truth and nobody wants to tell you. Well, Gino Giovani the truth is you are my nephew ... and my son. The Don was married to my sister, Dorrita, until she died in a child birth with you.

GINO. (*Disappointed.*) My mother was your sister? (*Pause.*) Not a Third Avenue whore? Not a maid? Not a chorus girl?

CORRITA. (*Shakes her head "no" as every question.*) Disappointed?

GINO. (*Loving.*) No. No ... Mama.

(CORRITA and GINO hug.)

BABY. (*Sobbing.*) It's like being a part of daytime drama.

CONNIE. (*Impatient.*) Yeah, as the ravioli turns. Now who's the murderer?

CORRITA. The murderer is ... (*Stops looks around.*) Wait there's some more loose ends. (*Turns to Valaria and speaks to her.*) Real loose. Valaria was so upset when the thief, Roberto, took her purse because she said there were valuable bracelets in it. The only thing I found was an envelope of cash. An envelope with the Don's name and address.

VALARIA. The Don paid me a couple grand to stay away from Gino. Big deal.

GINO. (*Heartbroken.*) I thought you loved me?

(CONNIE and VALARIA break out laughing.)

CORRITA. SHUT UP! *(To Valaria.)* You said the Don sent you in tunnels because it was a short cut to the liquor store. How did you know which tunnel was the one that would get you there?

BABY. *(Realizing.)* She was really one of Papa's mistresses.

VALARIA. Yeah. I was. So what?

GINO. *(Angry.)* You slept with my father?

VALARIA. He was a hellva lot better than you.

CORRITA. Get outta my house.

GINO. *(In shock.)* You slept with my father?

VALARIA. *(To Corrita.)* May I please have my handbag?

(CORRITA hands it to her.)

VALARIA. I trust my envelope is in there?

CORRITA. Of course.

(VALARIA musters up dignity and crosses to the stairs.)

CONNIE. Why can't I trash her face, Mama?

(VALARIA exits.)

CORRITA. 'Cause you're a lady. 'Cause you got dignity, respect and integrity.

(CORRITA produces the money that was in the envelope and tosses it in the air. ALL laugh.)

CORRITA. I didn't lie. The envelope is in her purse.

CONNIE. Mama, you're worse than us.

GINO. (*Appalled.*) She slept with Papa?

CORRITA. (*Slaps Gino in the back of his head.*) Get over it!

CONNIE. I can't stand the suspense no more. Who the hell killed the old man?

CORRITA. Don't you know, Connie?

CONNIE. I wouldn't be asking if I knew, would I?

CORRITA. I never thought any of my children, no matter what they might have said in anger, could kill the man who gave them life. I raised my kids better than that. There was only one person who could commit this crime.

CONNIE and ONE-EYED JOE. Who?

CORRITA. A person who deceived us all ...

GINO. Who?

CORRITA. ... with a plan so ....

ROBERTO and BABY. Who?

CORRITA. ... perfect it couldn't fail.

CONNIE. For God's sake old woman would you just tell us.

CORRITA. Rocky Studds Malone.

CONNIE. Rocky?

GINO. Rocky's dead, Mama.

ONE-EYED JOE. That's right.

CORRITA. Is he?

ONE-EYED JOE. That's what everyone says.

CONNIE. I won't believe it. He promised me he wouldn't ever kill, Papa. For the fifteen years Rocky and I dated he had thousands of opportunities to bump Papa off, but he didn't. He didn't 'cause he knew I loved my father.

CORRITA. You brought Rocky into this house, Connie. You gave him the opportunity to learn the tunnels. At any given time he had access to this room and the information kept here. You slept with the enemy in this very room.

CONNIE. Rocky Studds Malone died months ago.

CORRITA. Nick the Fish is dead. I ask myself why? Nick wasn't a hood. Sure all his friends were but he wasn't. He only did business with us.

GINO. What does that got to do with the clues?

BABY. The make-up, the glove, the gu ...

CORRITA. (*Pulls out a can of fish oil. Interrupting/adding.*) The fish oil.

ROBERTO. Fish oil?

CORRITA. Roberto, go smell the back of Connie's neck.

CONNIE. What?

(ROBERTO does so.)

CORRITA. Everywhere you went, Connie, you complained that your husband smelled like fish 'cause he collected protection money on the wharf.

ROBERTO. Yeah. She stinks. There's fish oil on her neck.

CONNIE. What!

CORRITA. But One-eyed Joe here smells like *Surrender* perfume. I ask myself why? Maybe One-Eyed Joe used to smell like fish. Maybe you got used to associating him with the smell of fish whether he was there or not. It was all apart of Rocky's plan. (*Turns to One-Eyed Joe.*) Isn't that right ... ROCKY!

CONNIE. WHAT!?!?!?

(Each turns toward ONE-EYED JOE/ROCKY)

GINO. ROCKY?
BABY. Studds?
ROBERTO. Malone?

(ROCKY removes the gray wig, the fake nose, the eye patch and stands completely erect.)

CONNIE. Oh, God.

CORRITA. He said Nick the Fish recommended him for Connie's groom. Nick was killed so the story couldn't be checked. He knew all about the tunnels and where they led. The make-up was from his disguise. Because he's so athletic he was able to run upstairs enter the tunnels from there, then climb down the ladder, shoot Papa and get back before he was missed.

ROCKY/JOE. *(Angry.)* Yeah. That's right. But it was all for nothing. Huh, Connie? The Don died for nothing.

CONNIE. Oh, God.

ROCKY. *(Hatefully, ROCKY begins stalking Connie.)* For nothing. You don't want me. We've been playing a game for fifteen years. You never wanted me. You want the damn business. The business is all that matters to you. NOT ME!!!

CONNIE. *(Verge of tears.)* You promised me you wouldn't kill my father and you shot him in the back? Where's the honor in that?

ROCKY. *(Screaming.)* I lie. I cheat. I steal. I kill. I'm a crook.

CONNIE. You son-of-a-bitch!

ROCKY. Fifteen years I've waited for you. Fifteen years I've been crawling around tunnels playing hide and seek. For what? Did you ever love me?

CONNIE. (*Sad.*) I thought you were a man of honor. I made you promise not to kill my father 'cause I didn't want you. I've never loved you, Rocky.

ROCKY. (*In pain.*) ~~Jesus~~! You lied.

CONNIE. I'm a crook too. You never seemed to understand that.

ROCKY. If you didn't want to marry me and be my wife, why'd you keep me hanging around for so long, Connie?

CONNIE. You were the best ~~piece of~~ *lover* ass I ever had.

ROCKY. That's it?

CORRITA. Just like her Papa.

ROCKY. I loved you. (*Turns to Corrita.*) I ain't ever looked in the Don's desk or took any information outta this room, Corrita. I came here for love and nothing more. I got principles.

CONNIE. I'm sorry, Rocky.

ROCKY. Can I kiss you one last time, Connie Elaine?

CONNIE. Sure.

(ROCKY moves to her. ROBERTO comes between them.)

ROBERTO. Excuse me. As a poet. I appreciate and understand your tale of lies and love. It is poignant like the cry of the dove and truly a romantic tragedy, but hope springs eternal and perhaps in another life you will reunite—I know not. I do, however, ... (*Building.*) ...

KNOW THAT THIS MAN KILLED MY FATHER FOR
NO REASON!!!

*(ROBERTO slugs ROCKY in the chops, then in the gut
and then karate chops his back. ROCKY falls.)*

CONNIE. *(Puts her arm around Roberto.)* We're gonna
make you a true Giovani yet.

GINO. CAN I GET OUTTA THESE DAMN
HANDCUFFS????

CORRITA. Baby, help your brother.

CONNIE. What about Papa's will, Mama?

CORRITA. Yeah, well, there ain't no will. He left it
all to me, see.

GINO. What?

CORRITA. The money, the house, the business, the
cars ... everything, Gino, is mine.

GINO. You're gonna run the business?

CORRITA. Tell you what, Gino. I'll give you the
money for your private business venture if you help your
sister, Connie, take control of the family business.

GINO. It's a deal.

CONNIE. Mafia QUEENDOM here I come!! *(CONNIE
exits.)*

CORRITA. Gino, Roberto get Rocky Studds Malone to
your Uncle Vito. Use the secret tunnel, it's quicker. Uncle
Vito will know how to dispose of him.

ROBERTO. What about my poetry?

BABY. And my acting?

CORRITA. Get help!

ROBERTO. *(Picking up Rocky with Gino. Reciting.)* I
feel life in his body as I lift it with my hands. Yet fleeting
is his life—like grains of sand. The sun is setting across
his brow. Death awaits though I know not how.

(ROBERTO and GINO move ROCKY's body and exit through the secret passageway. ROBERTO'S poem fades as the panel closes.)

BABY. Beat me, Beat me, Harder Harder ... Here I come!!!

(BABY exits. CORRITA grabs her suitcase and black purse and looks around.)

CORRITA. Donald. Oh, Donald. I have this terrible feeling you're rolling over in your grave. *(CORRITA looks up to the heavens as if to address the Don in heaven.)* My little meatball man, I gotta admit ... *(SHE stops, thinks deeply and then looks down realizing the Don is probably in hell. Sweet and soft.)* My little meatball man, I gotta admit that I'm gonna miss you very much. We had some good times. You made living an adventure. But, Donnie ... *(Turns sarcastic and bitter.)* ... after forty years of doing everything you always wanted to do I'm finally gonna do whatever the hell I wanna do. *(CORRITA reaches into the purse and takes out sunglasses and Mickey Mouse ears.)* I'm going to Disney World.

(A moment of silence.)

THE DON'S VOICE. *(Ghostly, but unmistakable.)* No, you ain't 'cause I'm gonna haunt you till you die, woman.
CORRITA. *(Trembling.)* Mama mia!

(THE DON'S laughter.)

BLACKOUT

END OF PLAY

COSTUME PLOT

CONNIE ELAINE
I, 1:
Red sexy dress
I, 2:
Leopard print hat,
Leopard print coat,
Black dress
I, 3:
White wedding dress (mini skirt with too many bows),
High fashion white hat with long veil,
Extra large white hand bag
ROCKY STUDDS MALONE
I, 1:
GQ-styled dark pin-striped suit
White shirt
AS ONE-EYED JOE PROVOLONE
I, 2:
Sloppy ill-fitting suit
Light gray tuxedo with pink shirt
BABY GIOVANI
I, 1:
Dress Marilyn Monroe wore in *Seven Year Itch*
I, 2:
A neon green Muu Muu
I, 3:
A pink bridesmaid's dress
CORRITA GIOVANI
I, 1 & 2:
Black plain dress
Black handbag (never without it)
Black "old lady" shoes
Drooping stockings
I, 3:

Pink plain dress
Black handbag
Black "old lady" shoes
Drooping stockings
ROBERTO GIOVANI
I, 1 & 2:
White, stained oxford button-down shirt
60's large bowtie.
Tight pants – too short in the legs (floods)
White socks with black penny loafers
I, 3:
Over-sized gray tuxedo with pink shirt
VALARIA CONSTANTINE
I, 1:
Black lace mini dress! Gaudy!
I, 3:
Tramp-like gold mini dress
Gold hat and pink clutch purse
GINO GIOVANI
I, 1 & 2:
Dark suit
I, 3:
Light gray tuxedo with pink shirt
DONALD GIOVANI
I, 1 & 2:
Dark suit
I, 3:
Light gray tuxedo with pink shirt

In ACT II all characters stay in their ACT I Scene 3
costumes.

PROPERTY PLOT

Accessories for the bar
Accessories for the Don's desk
A cake
Presents
Red and white checkered tablecloth
Bags of potatoes chips, pretzels, etc.
Baskets for above
Jar of nuts
A steaming pot of soup
A spray can of whipped cream
Cigarettes
A credit card
Two guns
A white ski mask
Gino's briefcase and 976 papers
Broken tennis racket
An envelope
An 8 x 10 photo of Rocky
Phone on desk
Banker's lamp on desk
A black glove
Pair of handcuffs
A Will
Large cloth bag
Can of fish oil
Hot pink sunglasses
Mickey Mouse ears
Suitcase
Stack of paper money
Roll of masking tape
Books

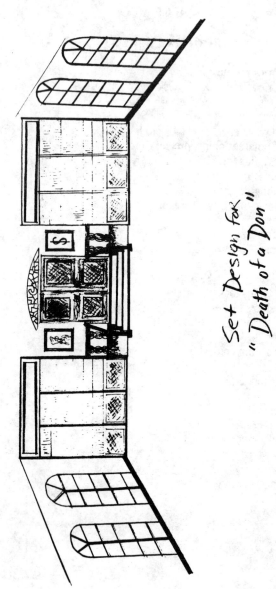

Set Design for
"Death of a Don"

By RONALD KANUE MYRROH '92

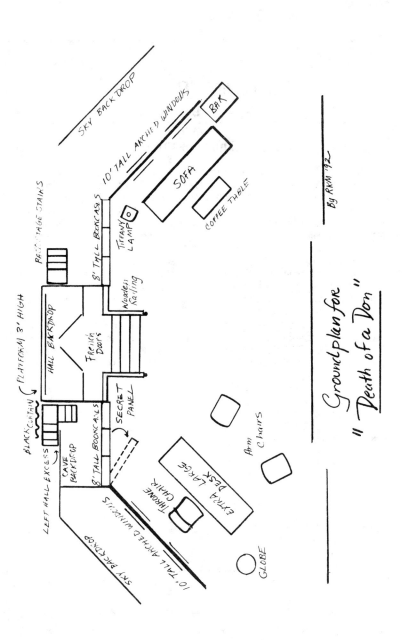

Groundplan for
"Death of a Don"

By RKM '92

CEMENTVILLE
by Jane Martin
Comedy
Little Theatre

(5m., 9f.) Int. The comic sensation of the 1991 Humana Festival at the famed Actors Theatre of Louisville, this wildly funny new play by the mysterious author of *Talking With* and *Vital Signs* is a brilliant portrayal of America's fascination with fantasy entertainment, "the growth industry of the 90's." We are in a run-down locker room in a seedy sports arena in the Armpit of the Universe, "Cementville, Tennessee," with the scurviest bunch of professional wrasslers you ever saw. This is decidedly a small-time operation—not the big time you see on TV. The promoter, Bigman, also appears in the show. He and his brother Eddie are the only men, though; for the main attraction(s) are the "ladies." There's Tiger, who comes with a big drinking problem and a small dog; Dani, who comes with a large chip on her shoulder against Bigman, who owes all the girls several weeks' pay; Lessa, an ex-Olympic shotputter with delusions that she is actually employed presently in athletics; and Netty, an overweight older woman who appears in the ring dressed in baggy pajamas, with her hair in curlers, as the character "Pajama Mama." There is the eager-beaver go-fer Nola, a teenager who dreams of someday entering the glamorous world of pro wrestling herself. And then, there are the Knockout Sisters, refugees from the Big Time but banned from it for heavy-duty abuse of pharmaceuticals as well as having gotten arrested *in flagrante delicto* with the Mayor of Los Angeles. They have just gotten out of the slammer; but their indefatigable manager, Mother Crocker ("Of the Auto-Repair Crockers") hopes to get them reinstated, if she can keep them off the white powder. Bigman has hired the Knockout Sisters as tonight's main attraction, and the fur really flies along with the sparks when the other women find out about the Knockout Sisters. Bigman has really got his hands full tonight. He's gotta get the girls to tear each other up in the ring, not the locker room; he's gotta deal with tough-as-nails Mother Crocker; he's gotta keep an arena full of tanked-up rubes from tearing up the joint—and he's gotta solve the mystery of who bit off his brother Eddie's dick last night. (#5580)

THE BABY DANCE
Little Theatre-Drama
by Jane Anderson

3m., 2f. 2 Ints. Stephanie Zimbalist starred in the original production of this brilliant, moving new drama, both at the Pasadena Playhouse and at the Long Wharf Theatre. She played a woman from Los Angeles named Rachel who has everything she wants in life—except a child. Rachel has located a poor couple who have more children than they can afford to keep, and have agreed to let their latest, when it is born, be adopted by Rachel and her husband. Desperate for a healthy baby, Rachel is paying for all of the poor woman's pre-natal care and hospital expenses. When she arrives for a visit at the trailer park where Al and Wanda live, she is appalled to find that Wanda is not eating correctly. She is also appalled by Al, who actually comes on to her when he is not seething with resentment. The whole arrangement nearly falls through, but by the second act, both couples are back on track. Until, that is, it is learned that the newborn baby may—just may—have suffered some brain damage in the difficult birth, causing Wanda's husband to back away from the deal, much to Rachel's chagrin. Rachel wants the baby anyway, wants to take the chance. In the end, the childless couple do renege on the deal, leaving Wanda and Al with yet another mouth to feed. "The best play produced this season at the Long Wharf Theatre and the first in several seasons to touch the heart so profoundly."—New Haven Advocate. *"The Baby Dance* is not just a 'woman's play.' It is a gripping drama that leaves the audience with more empathy for these people than they would have thought possible."—Bridgeport Post. "A powerful, deeply wrenching drama."—Berkshire Eagle. "It would take a heart of stone to be unmoved by Jane Anderson's *The Baby Dance*.". (#4305)

THE BATTLE OF SHALLOWFORD
Little Theatre-Comedy
by Ed Simpson

8m., 1f. Int. On a quiet Sunday night, the local regulars have gathered at Burton Mock's general store, in the small town of Shallowford, NC. It is October, 1938. The rest of the world is poised on the brink of war, but the locals aren't much worried about events in the world at large. They're more interested in the local gossip—and Burton's general store is the best place to hear it. The regulars include the gossipy, whining Clunette; fey church choirmaster Fred; lowlife, wild-eyed Newsome Jarvis, on hand with his "slow" son, Doodad; Mr. Roy, a one-armed World War I veteran who holds court at the store; egotistic local football hero Dewey Sowers; Burton's restless young daughter, Ruthie; and her schoolmate Lonny Hutchins, a sci-fi aficionado. All is calm; until, that is, they turn on the radio and learn that the Martians have invaded! Of course, it is the famous Orson Welles broadcast they are listening to—but they fall for it hook, line and shotgun, and run out to do battle against the fearsome threat from the invading Martians. Only Lonny suspects that something is fishy, but he's got his hands full if he thinks he's gonna deter the local yokels from their moment of glory. This delightful new comedy has had several successful productions nation-wide, and is finally available to y'all. Read it if you want a good laugh; produce it if that's how you like your audience to respond. "A theatrical gem."—Asheville Citizen-Times. "Tickle their funny bones, warm their hearts, don't insult their intelligence ... Ed Simpson's *The Battle of Shallowford* hits that magic trio."—Knoxville News-Sentinel. "A sentimental comedy that's hilariously on target. It could easily become a community theatre staple in much the way the works of Larry Shue have."—Knoxville Journal. A cassette tape of excerpts from the Mercury Theatre's radio broadcast of "The War of the Worlds" called for in the text of the play is available for $10, plus postage. (#4315)

LEND ME A TENOR
(Farce)
by KENNETH LUDWIG

4 male, 4 female

This is the biggest night in history of the Cleveland Grand Opera Company, for this night in September, 1934, world-famous tenor Tito Morelli (also known as "Il Stupendo") is to perform his greatest role ("Otello") at the gala season-opening benefit performance which Mr. Saunders, the General Manager, hopes will put Cleveland on the operatic map. Morelli is late in arriving--and when he finally sweeps in, it is too late to rehearse with the company. Through a wonderfully hilarious series of mishaps, Il Stupendo is given a double dose of tranquilizers which, mixed with all the booze he has consumed, causes him to pass out. His pulse is so low that Saunders and his assistant, Max, believe to their horror that he has died. What to do? What to do? Max is an aspiring singer, and Saunders persuades him to black up, get into Morelli's Otello costume, and try to fool the audience into thinking that's Il Stupendo up there. Max succeeds admirably, but the comic sparks really fly when Morelli comes to and gets into his other costume. Now we have *two* Otellos running around, in costume, and two women running around, in lingerie -- each thinking she is with Il Stupendo! A sensation on Broadway and in London's West End. "A jolly play."--NY Times. "Non-stop laughter"--Variety. "Uproarious! Hysterical!"--USA Today. "A rib-tickling comedy."--NY Post. (#667) **Posters.**

POSTMORTEM
(Thriller)
by KENNETH LUDWIG

4 male, 4 female . Int.

Famous actor-manager and playwright William Gillette, best known for over a generation as Sherlock Holmes in his hugely-successful adaptation of Conan Doyle (which is *still* a popular play in the Samuel French Catalogue), has invited the cast of his latest revival of the play up for a weekend to his home in Connecticut, a magnificent pseudo-medieval, Rhenish castle on a bluff overlooking the Connecticut River. Someone is trying to murder William Gillette, and he has reason to suspect that it is one of his guests for the weekend. Perhaps the murderer is the same villain who did away with Gillette's fiancee a year ago if you believe, as does Gillette, that her death was not--as the authorities concluded--a suicide. Gillette's guests include his current ingenue/leading lady and her boyfriend, his Moriarty and his wife, and Gillette's delightfully acerbic sister. For the evening's entertainment Gillette has arranged a seance, conducted by the mysterious Louise Perradine, an actress twenty years before but now a psychic medium. The intrepid and more than slightly eccentric William Gillette has taken on, in "real life", his greatest role: he plans to solve the case *a la* Sherlock Holmes! The seance is wonderfully eerie, revealing one guest's closely-guarded secret and sending another into hysterics, another into a swoon, as Gillette puts all the pieces of the mystery together before the string of attempts on his life leads to a rousingly melodramatic finale. " shots in the dark and darkly held secrets, deathbed letters, guns and knives and bottles bashed over the head, ghosts and hiders behind curtains and misbegotten suspicions. There are moments when you'll jump. Guaranteed."--The Telegraph. (#18677)

WHAT THE BELLHOP SAW
(Little Theatre)
(FARCE)

by Wm. Van Zandt and Jane Milmore

8 male, 4 female

The play starts with a rather nice fellow checking into a $400.00 suite in "New York City's finest hotel". From there it snowballs into a fabulous nightmare involving a Salman Rushdie-type author, an Iranian Terrorist, a monstrous shrew-like woman, a conniving bellboy, a monumentally incompetent F.B.I. man, a nubile celebrity-mad maid, a dim-witted secretary, and a cute little pigtailed girl. All the while, gag lines are popping at Orville Redenbacher speed. Everything happens at pretty much whirlwind velocity. This latest farce by Van Zandt and Milmore combines topical humor with the traditional antics of farce: doors slamming, characters careening and confusion reigning supreme. A wildly funny farce! An excellent piece of workmanship by our two authors who take pride in the old-fashioned craft of comedy writing. #25062

◆◆◆◆◆◆◆◆◆◆◆◆◆◆◆◆◆◆◆◆◆◆◆◆◆◆◆◆◆◆◆◆

THE SENATOR WORE PANTYHOSE
(Little Theatre)
(COMEDY)

by Wm. Van Zandt and Jane Milmore

7 male, 3 female

If you're tired of political and religious scandals, this is your greatest revenge! Van Zandt & Milmore's latest comedy revolves around the failing Presidential campaign of "Honest" Gabby Sandalson, a regular guy whose integrity has all but crippled his bid for the White House. Desparate for votes, his sleazeball campaign manager trumps up an implausible sex scandal which accidentally backfires on PMS Club leader Reverend Johnny and his makeup-faced wife Honey Pie; an opportunistic innkeeper with a penchant for antique food; the town's wayward single girl; two escaped convicts looking for stolen loot; and newscaster Don Bother. "A guaranteed hit!" (Asbury Park Press) "The characters swap beds, identities and jabs in what may be a flawless sex farce." (The Register). #21084

MIXED FEELINGS
(Little Theatre—Comedy)

Donald Churchill
m., 2 f., Int.

This is a riotous comedy about divorce, that ubiquitous, peculiar institution which so shapes practically everyone's life. Arthur and Norma, ex-spouses, live in separate apartments in the same building. Norma has second thoughts about her on-going affair with Arthur's best-friend; while Arthur isn't so sure he wants to continue *his* dalliance with Sonia, wife of a manufacturer with amusingly kinky sexual tastes (Dennis—the manufacturer—doesn't mind that his wife is having an affair; just so long as she continues to provide him with titillating accounts of it while he is dressed as a lady traffic cop). Most of Sonia's accounts are pure fiction, which seems to keep Dennis happy. Comic sparks are ignited into full-fledged farcical flames in the second act, when Dennis arrives in Arthur's flat for lessons in love from the legendary Arthur! "Riotous! A domestic laught romp! A super play. You'll laugh all the way home, I promise you.'—Eastbourne News. "Very funny ... a Churchill comedy that most people will thoroughly enjoy."—The Stage. Restricted New York City.

THE DECORATOR
(Little Theatre/Comedy)

Donald Churchill
m., 2 f., Int.

Much to her surprise, Marcia returns home to find that her flat has not been painted, as she arranged. In fact, the job hasn't even been started yet. There on the premises is the housepainter who is filling in for his ill colleague. As he begins work, there is a surprise visitor--the wife of the man with whom Marcia is having an affair, who has come to confront her nemesis and to exact her revenge by informing Marcia's husband of his wife's infidelity. Marcia is at her wit's end about what to do, until she gets a brilliant idea. It seems the housepainter is a part-time professional actor. Marcia hires him to impersonate her husband, Reggie, at the big confrontation later that day, when the wronged wife plans to return and spill the beans. Hilarity is piled upon hilarity as the housepainter, who takes his acting *very* seriously, portrays the absent Reggie. The wronged wife decides that the best way to get back at Marcia would be to sleep with her "husband" (the house painter), which is an ecstatic experience for them both. When Marcia learns that the housepainter/actor/husband has slept with her rival, she demands to have the opportunity to show the housepainter what *really* good sex is. "This has been the most amazing day of my life", says the sturdy painter, as Marcia leads him into her bedroom. "Irresistible."—London Daily Telegraph.